D1649064

The American Dream

Jamestown and the Planting of the American Christian Republic

Stephen McDowell

And

Mark Beliles

PROVIDENCE FOUNDATION
CHARLOTTESVILLE, VIRGINIA

The American Dream:
Jamestown and the Planting of the American Christian Republic
By Stephen McDowell and Mark Beliles

Copyright © 2007 by Stephen McDowell and Mark Beliles
First printing, 2007

All rights reserved. No part of this book may be reproduced in any manner whatsoever without written permission of the publisher, except in the case of brief quotations in articles and reviews.

Published by:
Providence Foundation
PO Box 6759
Charlottesville, VA 22906
434-978-4535
Email: info@providencefoundation.com
www.providencefoundation.com

The Providence Foundation is a Christian educational organization whose purpose is to train and network leaders of education, business, and politics to transform their culture for Christ.

Cover picture: Stephen Reid (English, 1873-1948), *The Landing at Cape Henry, April 1607*, 1928, Oil on canvas, 50 x 62 inches. Courtesy of the Chrysler Museum of Art, Norfolk, VA, Gift of the Organizations and Citizens of Norfolk and vicinity in memory of Alethea Serpell, past President, Council of Assembly Tidewater Virginia Women, 35.14.1.

The American Dream. Chapters 1, 2, 3, 5, 6, and part of 4 were written by Stephen McDowell. Mark Beliles wrote part of Chapter 4 and compiled the two appendixes.

Printed in the United States of America

ISBN 1-887456-20-1

Table of Contents

The American Dream: Jamestown and the Planting of the American Christian Republic

The American Dream

"Wee shall by plantinge [in America] inlarge the glory of the gospell . . . and provide a safe and a sure place to receave people from all partes of the worlds that are forced to flee for the truthe of Gods worde."

Rev. Richard Hakluyt, 1584

"The American dream is that every man must be free to become whatever God intends he should become."

Ronald Reagan, 1971

Chapter 1

The Uniqueness of the United States in History

America is different than any nation in history. Her uniqueness can be seen from the time of colonization, through obtaining independence, to being established as a constitutional republic, and advancing greatly as a free nation. This nation was, and in many ways still is, special. America is the most free and prosperous nation to have ever existed. **America is exceptional.** This has nothing to do with any inherent value of the American people, but has to do with the valuable ideas upon which she was founded.

A few of the ideas incorporated into American society making it exceptional include: valuing the individual; freedom of worship; freedom of assembly; opportunity for all to labor and benefit from the fruit of their labor; freedom to elect representatives and have a voice in government; freedom of thought and expression of ideas; freedom to own property; freedom to obtain ideas, start businesses and create wealth; limited jurisdiction of civil government; equal standing before the law for all people; no class distinctions; the central role of the family. These are part of the *American Dream*.

These ideas produced great liberty, justice, prosperity, charity, virtue, and knowledge. They made America a success and made her powerful. This power and wealth has been used, not for conquest, but for good — for furthering liberty in the world. America has been a great blessing to the nations. Blessings have come from the private sector by giving aid, starting hospitals and schools, sending forth missionaries, and much more. The American government has also been a great blessing in assisting many nations who have fought against tyrants seeking to oppress them, and by sending large sums of money to nations encountering natural disasters and other threats.

Throughout America's history, people have flocked to her shores to experience the fruit of her liberty and prosperity — this like no other nation in history. Those that have come have been greatly blessed. Many have escaped persecution and experienced freedom to worship God and pursue their calling. Other nations, recognizing this exceptionalism, have sought to imitate the principles that made America great, and have, to some degree, benefited as well.

Early Americans recognized the special nature of the nation in history. John Adams said,

> I always consider the settlement of America with reverence and wonder, as the opening of a grand scene and design in Providence for the illumination of the ignorant, and the emancipation of the slavish part of mankind all over the earth.[1]

Historian B.F. Morris said: "God held this vast land in reserve, as the great field on which the experiment was to be made in favor of a civil and religious liberty."[2] Historian and leading educator of women, Emma Willard, stated: "In observing the United States, there is much to convince us, that an Almighty, Overruling Providence, designed from the first, to place here a great, united people."[3] Alexis de Tocqueville wrote:

> In that land the great experiment was to be made by civilized man, of the attempt to construct society upon a new basis; and it was there, for the first time, that theories hitherto unknown, or deemed impracticable, were to exhibit a spectacle for which the world had not been prepared by the history of the past.[4]

Many of the early colonizers of America came with the vision of establishing a unique nation in history. John Winthrop wrote of the Puritans' desire to be "A Model of Christian Charity,"— **"as a city upon a hill,"** where all the people of the earth would look upon and say of their own nation, "the Lord make it like that of New England."[5] William Penn said that God gave him the land that became Pennsylvania so that he could set up a model state — **"a holy experiment"** — "which should open its doors to every kindred" and be a refuge for men of all creeds.[6]

Pressure to Abandon Unique Founding Principles

America's founding principles made her unique, free, and powerful, but there are many today who would have her abandon those principles. There is a call for America to be like other nations. Some have said she should follow the directions of the United Nations or act like Europe, and in so doing we would then be civil, not stir up evil leaders, or cause other problems in the earth.

This call has come from other nations, but also from many in America, including the mainstream media, academia, and liberal politicians. It has come from those who either do not love liberty or those who are ignorant of what is necessary to produce and sustain a free and prosperous society. They proclaim we must be like other nations, but it is our becoming like other nations that has caused us to decline. (This is similar to what happened to Israel of old. The more Israel became like other nations, the more problems she had.)

We do not want to be like Europe or other nations. We had a revolution to escape the tyranny of Europe. The ideas incorporated in America subsequently helped to change Europe, and many other nations, for the better.

It is obvious to most people why we do not want to be like tyrannical or dictatorial nations, for in such nations there is no liberty, no justice, and no prosperity for all (though an elite few may prosper); there is much oppression and government control. Such nations often have much chaos or internal conflict and war. We do not want to be like Islamic nations either, for many reasons: there is no freedom of worship; there is little, if any, input by the people into their governments; women are not treated as equals to men; the economies are generally stagnant and without oil there would be little prosperity. These we do not want to imitate, but how about the progressive European nations?

Why should we not want to be like the secular/socialistic European nations? After all, they seem to have as much freedom and prosperity as America. While these Western nations are more free and prosperous than most other countries (and this is due to their being influenced by the same Christian principles that formed the foundation of the American Republic), there is still much difference between them and America (though as America becomes more socialistic this difference is diminishing).

America is the most prosperous nation in history. Our standard of living is higher than the socialist nations of Europe, as well as the rest of the world. European governments control and regulate the lives of their citizens much more than the American government does its citizens. Consequently, there is less liberty and less prosperity in these nations. Taxes are much higher, the per capita gross domestic product is lower, and the standard of living is lower for the average European compared to the average American. A recent study by Swedish economists found that "most Americans have a standard of living which the majority of Europeans will never come anywhere near." "The really prosperous American regions have nearly twice the affluence of Europe."[7] By some measures poor Americans are better off than average Europeans. For example, they "have more square feet in their dwelling places (1228, or 438.6 per person) than the average Western European household (967.5, or 395.7 per person). By European standards, poor U.S. households also have astonishingly high rates of home ownership (45.9 percent), car ownership (72.8 percent), cable or satellite TV hookups (62.6 percent), VCR or DVD player ownership (78 percent), and microwave ownership (73.3 percent)."[8]

The economists who did this study point out "that if the 15 Western European nations in the European Union together became a U.S. state, it would rank ahead of only four other states in terms of per capita GDP."[9] A major reason for this lower productivity is the statist/socialistic policies of the Western European nations. There are many examples revealing the failure of statist ideas. Some years ago the Socialists of France enacted legislation requiring a 35-hour work week. The intent was to force employers to hire the many unemployed, but it only resulted in more unemployment with stagnating wages for those who were employed. A government thinking it knew best how to regulate the marketplace only ended up messing up the marketplace. Things got so bad, the government had to recently rescind the law.[10]

Many European nations require citizens to register their televisions, with some collecting annual taxes on each TV owned. While this is bad enough, some of these nations even send officials to the homes to count each TV to make sure they are all reported. A number of these statist nations have an official list of approved names that parents must use when naming their newborn children. According to one news report, a woman in Norway was "jailed for giving her son a name not approved by the government." Kirsti Larsen was sent to jail for two days "for choosing the name *Gesher* for her son." Larsen said she was a Christian and that she believed God wanted her to name her son *Gesher*, which is the Hebrew word for *bridge*.[11]

Socialistic European nations, as well as the European Union as a whole, have the "Caesar mentality." This view that civil government is the ultimate authority on earth has plagued most nations since the time of the tower of Babel. Those citizens and rulers with this philosophy see, usually unconsciously, the government as God. It is their provider from cradle to grave, their savior in times of trouble, the solver of all their problems (if only the right people are in control); it is that which can bring peace and utopia. If something needs to be done or a problem needs to be fixed, then look to the government. It knows what is best for humans, with such things as socialized medicine, that assigns each citizen a doctor, sets the fees charged, and other detailed controls. It even knows what is best for pigs.

"England's farmers must keep their pigs happy with toys and straw or face a big fine," reports Reuters in London. "Farmers have been told to put a football, metal chains, or hay in their pigsties to provide 'environmental enrichment' and stop pigs from getting bored and attacking each other. Anyone breaking the rules faces a fine of up to 2,500 pounds." This law originated with the European Union and was adopted in Great Britain in recent years.[12]

Other statist policies have had much more serious consequences, especially to Christians. In recent years, many pastors and others have been jailed and punished for teaching what the Bible says about homosexuality. Others have been persecuted for seeking to teach their children at home.

True liberty exists where individuals and the divine institutions of family, church, and state are free to fulfill their Biblical purpose and responsibilities. If the civil government suppresses or usurps the authority of the individual, or family, or church, then liberty is diminished or lost. In much of socialistic Europe (as well as most of the world), the state usurps much of the control of education and property that God says belongs to the family. The result is loss of liberty. This has also been occurring more in the United States in recent times.

Problems in America Today

According to some people today, America is not the land of the free and the place of prosperity, but it is the source of much of the evil in the world, and is certainly no better off than many other nations. Why then do so many people still want to immigrate to America? They come legally and illegally by the millions, and myriads more would come if they could. Do they know something these pundits do not?

America does have problems today. Over the past few generations there has been an increase in crime, a breakdown of the family, an increase of social immorality, growth of taxes, declining educational skills, and government intrusion into private, family, and church life. These things are largely due to the nation rejecting the ideas upon which she was founded and embracing humanistic, immoral ideas — that is, trying to be like most of the nations throughout history. If we continue to throw off the foundational principles that produced the American Dream, and embrace man-centered philosophies we will see America decline.

We are removing the Ten Commandments from classroom walls, courthouses, and public life in general — and more importantly failing to teach the fundamental principles in these commandments to our children — but then wonder why our jails are being filled with people who steal, murder, and rape people. We teach that men are merely animals and then bemoan the societal result of men acting like animals.

Some people say that America's greatest threat today comes from those who believe the nation should be governed by God-given moral standards. After all, they say, we cannot mix God and government. But these are the official standards the Founders gave us, truths, according to the Declaration that are self-evident, "that all men are created equal, that they are endowed by their Creator with certain unalienable rights." These rights, derived from "the laws of nature and of nature's God" are part of the founding principles that produced the American Dream.

The Source of America's Founding Principles

America's founding principles made her exceptional, powerful, and free. They produced the American Dream. Where did these principles originate? How were they planted in the nation?

The founding of America is unique. It has no parallel in history. The nation started from scratch, by a people providentially prepared and greatly influenced by the Protestant Reformation. They were a people of the Book. The founding ideas came from the Bible. They are Christian in their origin. These ideas were released to many people through the printing of Bibles in the common languages that especially began to occur in the sixteenth century. The early settlers of America carried these seed ideas with them as they colonized the nation in the seventeenth and eighteenth centuries. These ideas were planted, grew, and began to bear great fruit. This seed determined the fruit of the American Christian Republic. It produced America as an exceptional nation, the most free and prosperous in history.

The 400th anniversary of the founding of Virginia, the first permanent English settlement, is an important event because this marks the planting of the first seed of America. The seed determines the fruit. In Virginia, we can see some of the seed that resulted in the American republic.

Why should we in 2007 seek to remember what happened in 1607? We should remember and celebrate because this is a starting place to see God's hand in the founding and to learn the ideas that made America powerful. We must remember so we can return America to its foundational ideas and keep it a place of liberty, truth, and prosperity. This is not only for our good, but also that of our posterity, and for those people throughout the world who seek to establish freedom in their nations.

The man most influential in the founding of the colonies, Rev. Richard Hakluyt, understood the unique providential purpose of America. He wrote in 1584 that, "Wee shall by plantinge there inlarge the glory of the gospell . . . and provide a safe and a sure place to receave people from all partes of the worlds that are forced to flee for the truthe of Gods worde."[13]

His ideas were written into the First Charter of Virginia (1606):

> "We, greatly commending, and graciously accepting of, their Desires for the Furtherance of so noble a Work, which may, by the Providence of Almighty God, hereafter tend to the Glory of his Divine Majesty, in propagating of Christian Religion to such People, as yet live in Darkness and miserable Ignorance of the true Knowledge and Worship of God, and may in time bring the Infidels and Savages, living in those parts, to human Civility, and to a settled and quiet Government: DO, by these our Letters Patents, graciously accept of, and agree to, their humble and well-intended Desires."[14]

America's Providential Purposes

God had a purpose for America. Part of His providential purposes are seen in Hakluyt's writings, and include:

1. Inlarge the glory of the Gospel — that is, be a nation that produces the fruit of obedience to God's truth (which is liberty, justice, prosperity, charity, virtue, and knowledge) and then spread that truth throughout the world.

2. Be a place of refuge and freedom for the persecuted from many nations.

3. Be an example of liberty — all kinds of liberty: personal, religious, civil, economic, political.

4. Propagate the Gospel to the lost.

To fulfill the providential purposes of America and to make the American Dream a reality for ourselves and our posterity, we must remember what God has done in our history, repent of our apathy and ignorance, prepare ourselves and all citizens in the ideas that made us powerful, and return our nation to its original Godly covenant. This begins by understanding the story of the American Dream.

Chapter 2

Seven Ideas that Made America a Success

The seed principle is a common idea in Scripture. The Bible teaches that the Kingdom of God is like a seed (Mark 4:30-32). The seed determines the fruit, in nature and also in the sphere of ideas. Ideas determine what a culture or nation will be. Contrary to what modern academia may teach, all ideas are not the same. Therefore, all nations are not the same, since their foundational ideas have differed. Some nations have more liberty, prosperity, justice, and virtue than others. The Bible teaches, and history confirms, that the most free and prosperous nations are those that have most embraced the following seven ideas.

Rooted in the Bible, these ideas were expressed in different ways and had different degrees of influence in many nations from the first century through the establishment of America. The printing of the Bible in the common language of the people allowed these ideas to spread to many people and was the primary cause of the Protestant Reformation. These ideas, and the people who embraced them, brought change in parts of Europe, but had the greatest expression in America. Some European nations killed and drove out the seed of reform, like France and Spain. Other nations, as they went through revolution, alternately embraced and then persecuted reformers, like England. America was the greatest recipient of the good seed that came from many different nations. This seed was planted and grew in America. In addition, the seed of liberty developed more fully in America and its good fruit was seen in government, education, economics, family life, and all spheres.

These ideas produced varying amounts of fruit in various European nations. The most fruit came in those nations that most embraced Biblical ideas (like England, Holland, Germany, and Switzerland). Less fruit came forth in nations where the people had less access to the Bible (the source of these ideas). The fruit of these ideas was most evident and abundant in America. The fuller expression of these ideas in America also served as an example for Europe to progress even further in liberty and prosperity.

Western civilization advanced as these ideas took root and grew; yet, today much of the Western world is turning aside from these principles, resulting in loss of liberty and stagnation. Western Europe is much further down the road than America, but the more quickly this nation throws off the source of its success, the more quickly it will decline. To preserve liberty and to advance, America must embrace the seven following ideas, for they are what made her a success in the first place.

1. The Christian Idea of God (Theology)

The most important thing about a person is his view of God. The most important thing about a society is its view of God. This is true because we become like who, or what, we worship. A people are always moving toward their image of God. Since Christianity is the revealed truth of the Creator, cultures embracing Christianity have moved toward the true image and nature of God and the true state of reality within His universe. God has revealed Himself in His Creation (the law of nature) and more specifically in the Holy Scriptures — the revealed Word of God (the law of nature's God). Knowing and embracing the nature, character, and attributes of God affect individual lives as well as every aspect of society and culture.

The Christian's view of God is derived from the Bible, which presents an image of the Almighty living God — One who is omnipotent, omniscient, and omnipresent; a God of justice; yet, one who is forgiving, merciful, and loving. The true nature of God could never be created by the mind of man.

Man has made up all kinds of images of God. He looks many different ways to different people: He is like man, but bigger and stronger; He is harsh and stern, and sends judgment; He is found in rocks and trees and other parts of His creation; He is loving, gentle, not condemning, and allows all kinds of behavior (especially the evil things men want to do); he wants government to be his savior and provide all his needs.

"I made God in my mind," is the essence of humanism and man-made religions. Christians need to be careful of creating their own image of God. We cannot put God in a box.

A foundational component of Who He is — and of Christianity — is understanding the person of Jesus. He is Lord and Christ, and sovereign over all Creation. He is fully God, yet fully man; though, unlike all others, a perfect man (and as man He mercifully veiled His Godhood least we be overwhelmed). He is seated at the right hand of God, "far above all rule and authority and power and dominion . . . in this age [and] the one to come" (Eph. 1:20-23). All things are under His feet, in subjection to Him. He is the head over all things.

A few unique aspects of the true God include:

(1) The Triune nature of God

The Trinity is a fundamental doctrine of Christianity. There are three "persons" that comprise the Godhead — the Father is God, the Son is God, and the Holy Spirit is God. The triune nature of God has many implications for mankind and for all creation. One, it reveals there is a unity with diversity in creation. All creation is unified because we have a common Creator; the creation reflects the Creator. Yet, there is great diversity with that unity. For example, all men are alike in many ways. We are all created in the image of God, we all have similar physical, mental, and spiritual features that set us apart from all other aspects of creation — there is unity among men. Yet, no two humans are alike. Each has unique external physical characteristics (like fingerprints, voiceprints) and internal characteristics (like talents, skills, attitudes, callings) — there is diversity among men. This is true because we reflect our Creator and He is a picture of diversity. The Lord our God is one (unity), yet He manifests Himself in three "persons" (diversity).

Christian societies will recognize the unity with diversity of its citizens and encourage each to develop their talents and skills so as to pursue the fulfilling of their unique calling. This has implications in the economy, promoting prosperity through division and specialization of labor, and many other areas.

The nature of the Godhead also provides an example to mankind of love and service. The Son serves the Father, the Spirit carries out the wishes of the Son and Father, the Father lifts up the Son, and so on. Love is demonstrated by each member of the Godhead, which serves as an example of how man should act toward his fellow man. This idea is not presented by religions with a monotheistic view (like Islam) and less love and service to one another is historically seen in these nations compared to more Biblical societies.

(2) Justification by faith, not by our works

In contrast to Christianity, all religions are works oriented. Thus, people say certain prayers or mantras to help themselves or others. Some lash their backs to show they are willing to suffer to follow their god. Some carve idols from stones and logs and worship them with ceremonies. Some attempt to gain right standing with their god by killing the infidels, not for any crime against life, but merely because the infidels do not believe in their god. Often the civil laws reflect their concept of justification, and these laws restrict freedom of worship, speech, assembly, and other liberties that in a Christian society are recognized and protected as God-given. Christian societies do not see the law as the tool for justification and salvation. Law cannot save man. Only Christ's redeeming work can save man, and this free gift of God is received by faith, not by works. Man's view of justification affects the laws of a society.

(3) The priesthood of the believer

We can and must know God ourselves. This idea motivated Luther to put the Bible in the common language of the people, and to write hymns in the common language — that all may know Him personally. This idea affects civil life in many ways. One, it leads to the promotion of education for all people, because everyone has the right and responsibility to know God and His law-word for themselves. It also promotes democratic principles in a nation where each person has a voice in public affairs.

These are just a few of the concepts of God that separate Christianity from other religions. The Christian idea of God has had immense implications in many areas, including the development of the remaining six ideas.

The Founders of America believed that Christianity produced liberty. This belief arose from their Biblical worldview and from their knowledge of history. Our Founders believed that it was not just faith in any god or religion that formed the foundation of free societies, but it was specifically the Christian religion and faith in the only true God and His Word, the Bible. In a letter to James Madison from 16 October 1829, Noah Webster wrote:

> The christian religion, in its purity, is the basis or rather the source of all genuine freedom in government. . . . I am persuaded that no civil government of a republican form can exist & be durable, in which the principles of that religion have not a controlling influence.[1]

The father of American geography, Jedidiah Morse wrote: "To the kindly influence of Christianity we owe that degree of civil freedom, and political and social happiness which mankind now enjoys."[2] The U.S. House of Representatives declared in 1854: "[T]he great vital and conservative element in our system is the belief of our people in the pure doctrines and divine truths of the gospel of Jesus Christ."[3]

The Christian idea of God produced liberty in the world, all kinds of liberty — personal, religious, civil, and economic. Only where the Spirit of God is, is their liberty (2 Corinthians 3:17). Non-Biblical views of God have produced different fruit.

2. The Christian Idea of Man

Who is man? What are we? Are we fundamentally good? Are we mere bodies? Are we just like animals?

If we are just matter, then we are no different than bugs. It means nothing to squash human beings if you have such a view of man. Governments and leaders throughout history have had this view and have squashed many. In the twentieth century alone secular governments killed well over 100 million of their own citizens, and thought nothing of it.

A dominant view today is that men are an accident that crawled out of the primordial ooze; men are merely grown-up worms. However, God declares, all **men have great value**. They are important and special. Why? Man is created in the image of God (Gen. 1). This gives him value and worth. Men are equal in regards to their standing before God and the law, with certain God-given unalienable rights — life, liberty, and property. God Himself became a man (John 15), and could because man was made in His image, and through the person of Christ paid the price to redeem mankind. This added to the great value of man.

The Christian idea of man says that each man has an important calling and destiny that contributes to God's overall plan in history. Each person has an important contribution to make in bringing life to men and nations, in training posterity, in advancing the economy, and so on. This idea has had great effect in many areas, including economics, invention, business, and the medical field.

The Christian idea of man motivated Joseph Lister to develop antiseptic surgery, which has saved millions and millions of lives in the past century and a half. This idea also influenced Florence Nightingale's work in establishing modern nursing. Cyrus McCormick's desire to elevate the common farmer and empower him to prosper helped motivate him to invent the reaper, which has done more to eliminate famine in the earth than any other action of man. The Christian faith and the high regard George Washington Carver had for individuals inspired him to discover many agricultural advancements that greatly benefited farmers in America and throughout the world.

A society with a Christian view of man will seek to protect all life, not just those who are "important" or can contribute to the political fabric. This view breaks down class systems or castes.

While all men have great value, the Christian idea of man also reveals that **man is sinful** and in a fallen state. We are in need of a redeemer. We cannot save ourselves. We cannot live up to the standards of God.[4] We need the regenerating power of the Holy Spirit to work in us so that we might be delivered from the domain of darkness and born into the kingdom of light. Once we become a new creation we must grow in salvation — we must be sanctified in God's truth so we can go and extend His kingdom, His government, His truth in the nations. Biblical education is central in doing this.

Seeing man as sinful will affect how we live and conduct our societal affairs. One consequence is that we will not entrust man with too much power, because sinful man will tend to abuse power. We should bind down rulers with a constitution, hold them accountable with frequent elections, divide the legislative, executive, and judicial powers, and set up checks and balances within these separated governing bodies. Thus, a people's view of man affects their form of civil government. It will also affect their execution of justice, which should be swift but fair.

Without a Christian idea of man, society will see no difference between humans and animals. If man is just an animal, then his life is expendable. University of Texas biologist Eric Pianka was named the 2006 Distinguished Texas Scientist by the Texas Academy of Science. In his acceptance speech he reflected the humanistic view of man held by most of academia today, declaring "We're no better than bacteria!" He said that the planet is in danger from too many people and to alleviate the problem the human population must be reduced by 90 percent. War and famine are not killing enough people; disease is a better mechanism, but AIDS is not working fast enough. What is needed, according to this "distinguished" scientist, is to release an airborne variety of Ebola. This Central African virus kills rapidly by liquefying the internal organs. He estimates such action would have his desired results of killing about 90% of those who plague the world.[5]

Such an absurd idea follows logically from seeing man as a mere accident of nature. With regard to value, to those with a pagan view of man, a bacteria is a rat is a dog is a man. There is no difference, and we should think nothing of eliminating any men who are seen as a threat to the future of the world. This is why Hitler, Stalin, Mao, and other pagan thinkers could wipe out tens of millions of their own citizens without any second thought. But if we believe what modern "intellectuals" teach, how can we condemn such tyrants? It is the Christian idea of man that has protected life and advanced society.

3. The Christian Idea of the Family

The family is the basic building block of society. As the family goes, so goes the nation. The state of the family determines the state of the church, education, business, arts, civil government, and life. The home is the first sphere of society.

The true idea of family is realized only in the context of Christianity. Christianity defines the family's mission, purpose, and nature; plus it gives principles for strong and successful families. Simply stated, the purpose of the family is to be fruitful, to multiply, and take dominion over the earth (Gen. 1:28). The family is the institution that God created to provide education, health, and welfare for all its members.

From a Christian perspective a family is one man, one woman, and children who are related by marriage, blood, or adoption. The ideal family has a man and woman who covenant together to fulfill God's desire to be fruitful and bless the world. Both parents are to fulfill the purposes and responsibilities for and within the family, yet each has a unique role in fulfilling this mission.

In a Christian family a unity exists between the husband and wife, yet with diversity. The unique characteristics of husband and wife include a unique purpose for each. In general, God calls man to lead in taking dominion of the earth; woman is to support man in this. She is also especially involved in training the next generation and making the home an example of the Kingdom of God on earth. In fact, it is through the husband and wife fulfilling their duties in the home that the Kingdom of God will be extended throughout the earth. A primary means by which men take dominion over the earth is through their divine occupation. It is in the home that children are prepared for their life work.

People have debated in recent years whether women can compete with men in public life. Certainly they can, but let us never forget that no one can compete with a mother in the home—no one can fill her place. As more mothers have left the home for the workforce in recent years, through choice or necessity, our nation has experienced more and more problems; for those who can best form the character of the next generation are having less and less input into the lives of their children—those who are the next generation. Neither the state, nor the school, nor even the church, can effectively replace mom or dad in the home.

God has given to the family the responsibility to govern property and children. The family, not civil government, is to control the property and education within a nation. Whoever controls the property within a society, controls the present; whoever controls education, controls the future. God has given the family the government of both; hence, it is the most powerful institution that exists. Any actions to undermine the family and its authority will undermine the well-being of a nation.

A Christian understanding of the family was the backbone of the American Republic. The engraving on the base of the Pilgrim Mother Statue at Plymouth, Massachusetts, reflects the central influence of mothers, and hence families, in America:

> They brought up their families in sturdy virtue and a living faith
> in God without which nations perish.

If families in America do not continually pass on "sturdy virtue" and "a living faith in God," the nation will perish.

The Christian idea of the family has elevated women in history. It teaches that there is an equality between husband and wife, even though they have different roles. Where other views of the family have prevailed in the past, women were considered as lower members of society. This view is still evident today; as an example, there is no equality of men and women in Muslim nations.

Nations embracing the Christian view of the family have advanced in liberty, prosperity, justice, and virtue. Little or no advancement has occurred in those nations adhering to the eastern, communistic, or humanistic view of the family.

Under communism, the state attempted to assume much of the role of the family. (This is occurring in socialistic nations and secular western nations as well.) In the Ukraine, under communist rule, the government set up many state orphanages to care for many of her children. (The policies of the communist government produced a large number of orphaned children.) They thought having good medical care, food, and a comfortable physical building would be the best alternative family for needy young people; that meeting physical needs was really all these orphans needed, and the state could best provide this. However, they did not understand that loving parents with a peaceful, ordered environment are essential in building good citizens. The state's plan did not work and produced problems that are still evident today.

As Western Europe today has become more secular, families have begun to break down. In many nations children are told to report to the government if they are disciplined by their parents not according to secular standards. Many nations have laws forbidding parents to spank their children. Among other things, these humanistic ideas have led to disorder within the family and a decline in respect for parents and authority. Even Christian families are affected by this environment. One European Christian family was appalled to see an America father tell his son to do a small task for him, for they thought the father should only appeal to the son and let him decide if he obeyed or not.

America has been moving toward the statist European idea of the family. Legislation has been presented in California to outlaw spanking. The schools and state are acting more and more like the family (providing education and controlling property). The model of state education also diminishes the authority of the family in that grouping peers together for the first dozen years of schooling gives far too much influence to the peer group in shaping character and thought, when the family and mature mentors would be much more beneficial in shaping the next generations.

God intends the family to be the primary shapers of posterity. Only the family can effectively pass on the seeds of liberty and the Kingdom of God to future generations. It is important to realize that the foundation for self and civil government is laid in the families of a nation. Noah Webster wrote in *A Manual of Useful Studies:*

> In the family are formed the elements of civil government; the family discipline is the model of all social order; . . . the respect for the law and the magistrate begins in the respect for parents. . . . Families are the nurseries of good and bad citizens. The parent who neglects to restrain and govern his child, or who, by his example, corrupts him, is the enemy of the community to which he belongs; the parent who instructs his child in good principles, and subjects him to correct discipline, is the guardian angel of his child, and the best benefactor of society.[6]

An early President of the Continental Congress, Elias Boudinot, agreed:

> Good government generally begins in the family, and if the moral character of a people once degenerates, their political character must soon follow.[7]

Families recognizing their Biblical role will have a great impact in the future of a nation. As an example, Jonathan and Sarah Edwards faithfully discipled and educated their eleven children. In turn, their children passed on to future generations the vision for advancing liberty and building up their nation. A study was done of 1400 descendants of Jonathan and Sarah. Of these, 13 were college presidents, 65 were professors, 100 lawyers, 30 judges, 66 physicians, and 80 holders of public office including 3 senators, 3 governors, and a vice president of the United States. Their training not only benefited their children, but thousands of their descendants, and the nation at large.

The seeds we plant today through the training of our children will have impact beyond measure in the future. After all, one can count how many seeds are in an apple, but one cannot count how many apples are in a seed.

4. The Christian Idea of Truth (Law)

How do we know what we know? What is the basis for what we consider true and right?

For Christians, the basis of truth is found in God's Word. It is what the Bible proclaims. Jesus prayed to the Father: "Your word is truth" (John 17:17). His Word is not just true, but it is truth (a noun). Truth is what Jesus teaches, and He taught men must obey all the Scripture (Matt. 5:17-19). The Bible is God's Word and the source of Truth to all men. The degree to which men and nations have applied God's Word to all of life, is the degree to which they have prospered, lived in liberty, and been blessed.

A Christian worldview proclaims that there is truth, there is right and wrong, there are absolutes that we can know. The secularist has a much different view of "truth." From a humanistic perspective there is no absolute truth. All so-called truths are relative. The relativist says: "Whatever I want to believe, I may believe. Whatever I think is *true* is *true* for me, and whatever you think is *true* is *true* for you. If you believe in a God as the source of truth, that's okay, but I don't believe in God or absolute truth; and you shouldn't force your view upon me or upon society."

Relativism is the predominant view of those in academia, the media, and western governments. But such a view is completely illogical. When someone says "there is no absolute truth," a simple question will reveal the absurdity of this position. Merely ask them, "Are you sure?" If they answer no, they have jettisoned their epistemology, acknowledging that they do not know for certain that there are no absolutes. If they answer yes, then they have affirmed the position that there are absolutes.

(After someone admits there are absolutes, the next point to consider is who is the source of those absolutes. For Christians, it is the Bible. For humanists, it is man, either as an individual or corporate man with the state expressing "truth" to society.)

The belief in the certainty of no absolutes is not logical. It contradicts itself. One who believes this is like the man who built his house upon the sand — it cannot stand up under pressure of storms (see Matthew 7:24-27). If a worldview is built on this presupposition, it will fall.

A Christian worldview teaches there is absolute truth, where God is right about everything, and He reveals the truth that man needs to know in His Word. Relativists will condemn Christians who believe in right and wrong as narrow-minded and bigoted. They say, "You should not see things as right and wrong. It is **wrong** to do this."

What they are really saying is that they do not want to face the reality of the Creator God — Who is the source of all right and wrong — and His standard of righteous living. They want to live life on their own terms. Hence, their theology, or worldview, follows their morality.

A pagan view of "truth" has captured the thinking of most of the world. Relativism is the dominant view of Americans today, even those Americans who claim to be Christians. Barna conducted a poll in the Spring of 2002. In a survey of adults and teenagers, people were asked if they believed that there are moral absolutes that are unchanging, or that moral truth is relative. 64% of adults said truth is relative to the person and situation. Among teenagers, 83% said moral truth is relative; only 6% said it is absolute. Among born-again Christians 32% of adults and 9% of teens expressed a belief in absolute truth. The number one answer as to what people believe is the basis for moral decisions was doing whatever feels right (believed by 31% of adults and 38% of teens).

Early Americans, who were mostly Christians, held to the Christian idea of truth, which was reflected in their laws and constitutions. They believed that there is fixed law that applies to everyone and is always true. God reveals His law in nature (the laws of nature) and by special revelation in the Bible (the laws of nature's God). The phrase Jefferson used in the Declaration of Independence — "the laws of nature and of nature's God" — had a well established meaning.[8]

An early civics textbook, *First Lessons in Civil Government* (1846) by Andrew Young, reveals the Founders' Biblical view of law:

> The will of the Creator is the law of nature which men are bound to obey. But mankind in their present imperfect state are not capable of discovering in all cases what the law of nature requires; it has therefore pleased Divine Providence to reveal his will to mankind, to instruct them in their duties to himself and to each other. This will is revealed in the Holy Scriptures, and is called the law of revelation, or the Divine law.[9]

This is in great contrast to the secular or socialist view of law, as revealed in the French *Declaration of Rights* (1794): "the Law . . . is the expression of the general will. . . . [T]he rights of man rests on the national sovereignty. This sovereignty . . . resides essentially in the whole people."[10] To the humanist, man is the source of law, of right and wrong. But if whatever man declares to be lawful is the standard for society, then everyone's fundamental rights are threatened, for a majority, or ruling dictator, can declare anyone to be an outlaw. Tyrants have done this throughout history, and tens of millions of people have been killed under this worldview.

The Christian view of law proclaims that all men have God-given inalienable rights, and the Bible states what those rights are. No man can take them away. All men are subject to God's higher law, rulers as well as common people. No man is above the law, nor is man the source of law. Hence, the rule of law originated in the western Christian world where the Christian idea of law prevailed. This Christian view of law produced the unique nature of American constitutionalism and law.[11]

5. The Christian Idea of Creation and History

God created all things and He has a purpose for His creation. His creation functions upon a set of laws, physical and moral, that He built into the fabric of His universe. We can and should discover those laws. As we apply them, we are taking dominion over the earth and bringing advancement to mankind. These laws touch all areas of life, from understanding the force of gravity to understanding the Biblical power and form of government.

This Christian view has enabled the greatest scientists in history to bring advancements in all fields of science. Most of these great men of science were also men of God, and for those few who were not, they were still almost all a product of Christendom. Some of these Christian scientists include: Johann Kepler, William Herschel, Isaac Newton, James Maxwell, Francis Bacon, Carolus Linneaus, Blaise Pascal, James Joule, Michael Faraday, John Herschel, Robert Boyle, Louis Agassiz, Lord Kelvin, Jedediah Morse, John Fleming, Joseph Lister, James Simpson, Matthew Maury, Nathaniel Bowditch, Ephraim McDowell, George W. Carver, and Crawford W. Long.[12]

In the following prayer, James Maxwell (1831-1879), Scottish physicist and mathematician, reflected the view these scientists had as they approached the study of the universe from God's perspective:

> Almighty God, Who has created man in Thine own image, and made him a living soul that he might seek after Thee, and have dominion over Thy creatures, teach us to study the works of Thy hands, that we may subdue the earth to our use, and strengthen the reason for Thy service.[13]

God has a purpose for His creation that has been unfolding throughout history. Events of history, all of which contribute to His purpose and plan for mankind, have not been occurring by chance, but under the direction of the Sovereign God. This is a providential view of history.

The Bible clearly teaches the providence and sovereignty of God. "He rules over the nations" (Psalms 22:28). "He makes the nations great, then destroys them; He enlarges the nations, then leads them away" (Job 12:23). "It is He who changes the times and the epochs; He removes kings and establishes kings" (Daniel 2:21). "The God who made the world . . . gives to all life and breath and all things; and He made from one, every nation of mankind to live on all the face of the earth, having determined their appointed times, and the boundaries of their habitation, that they should seek God" (Acts 17:24-27). As these Scriptures teach, God is the one who raises up nations. He determines their time of existence and even their boundaries. Though men in rebellion to God have formed their own cities and nations, God is still sovereign over them. He has demonstrated that sovereignty in different ways as He set about accomplishing His plan in history. He deals with nations in a way that is based on the heart of the inhabitants.

Historian Charles Rollin wrote that history proclaims "that God disposes all events as Supreme Lord and Sovereign; that He alone determines the fate of kings and the duration of empires; and that He transfers the government of kingdoms from one nation to another because of the unrighteous dealings and wickedness committed therein."[14]

In early America the doctrine of Providence was widely embraced — "that God rules in the affairs of men is as certain as any truth of physical science,"[15] so stated historian George Bancroft in an address to Congress in 1866. Even non-Christians believed in Providence, as evidenced in Benjamin Franklin's statement calling the Constitutional Convention to prayer in June, 1787.[16]

A providential view of history produces optimism as we look to the future and consider how to deal with problems in the world (such as supposed limited natural resources, overpopulation, or lack of enough food).

God ultimately directs history, but He has given man authority, power, and the ability to rule God's creation — to change and direct what happens in the earth. If things are bad or not right, we can change them. The Christian view of history has motivated those who have worked to end religious and civil oppression, to abolish slavery, to create the tools and ideas necessary to lift men out of poverty, and to provide education for all people.

These advancements have not occurred where other philosophies have been dominant. They could not occur, for example, where the fatalistic view of eastern philosophies have prevailed. In such a worldview, men are born in a set state or caste, and they can do nothing to get themselves out of it. They cannot change their destiny — whatever is meant to be, will be. But the Christian idea of history teaches that God uses individuals to change the course of history and the destiny of nations. Men can change things. They can overcome evil. In fact, God commands men to change anything contrary to His standard; He commands men to take dominion over the earth.

6. The Christian Idea of Government

All government begins in the heart of man with his ability (or inability) to direct, regulate, manage, and control his life. There are two spheres of government — internal and external. Internal government is self-government. External government occurs in the family, church, business, associations, and civil government. External spheres of government are a reflection of the degree of internal self-government a person or people possess. Internal government is causative to external government.

The flow of power in a Christian society is from the internal to the external, from the inside-out. All authority and power comes from God. It flows from Him into the heart and mind of man, and then out into the family, church, business, schools, and civil realm. This idea greatly affected the development of government in America. Elias Boudinot revealed a fundamental principle upon which America was founded:

> Another essential ingredient in the happiness we enjoy as a nation, and which arises from the principles of the revolution, is the right that every people have to govern themselves in such manner as they judge best calculated for the common benefit.[17]

This was a new concept, because during most of history people lived under "ruler's law," where the rulers made the laws and the people had no voice in the matter. However, in America, the people made the laws, and everyone, including the rulers, was subject to them.

America's Founders understood that a people cannot govern themselves in civil affairs if they do not govern their own lives well. Robert C. Winthrop, speaker of the U.S. House of Representatives from 1847-49, said in 1849:

> All societies of men must be governed in some way or other. The less they may have of stringent State Government, the more they must have of individual self-government. The less they rely on public law or physical force, the more they must rely on private moral restraint. Men, in a word, must necessarily be controlled either by a power within them, or by a power without them; either by the Word of God, or by the strong arm of man; either by the Bible or the bayonet.[18]

The basis of the ability for man to govern himself well is rooted in his being in subjection to a higher power. The Founders' firm commitment to God, as well as their commitment to govern their lives according to His laws as contained in the Bible, was the foundation for self-government in America. Examination of the scores of constitutions, compacts, and charters written in colonial America readily reveals that the source of their civil law was found in the Bible. For example, in the *Massachusetts Body of Liberties* (which was a precursor to our Bill of Rights), written by Rev. Nathaniel Ward in 1641, the Pentateuch (the first five books of the Bible) was the basis for its criminal code, and "in case of the defect of a law in any partecular [sic] case" the standard was "the word of God."[19] Often the colonists would quote directly from the Scriptures and give references to justify their civil laws as seen, for example, in the laws of the Pilgrims.[20]

Self-government is limited apart from God; therefore, the ability to govern well is limited where the people and leaders do not seek to govern themselves and their nation under God. George Washington said, "It is impossible to govern the universe without the aid of a Supreme Being."[21]

The Christian idea of government led to the establishment of the American Christian Constitutional Federal Republic. It was unique in history and was only possible because the citizens were self-governed.

As was mentioned earlier, it is important to realize that the foundation for self-government is laid in the families of a nation. Families must begin early teaching the principle of self-government. One night, many years ago I was teaching my son, who was then about 5 years old, about self-government.[22] I gave him a definition he could understand, telling him that "self-government is doing what you are supposed to do without anybody telling you." The next morning he woke me early, took me to his bedroom, pointed to his bed, which he had made up all by himself without anybody telling him to do so, and remarked: "Dad, I was being self-governed, wasn't I?" The transformation of nations begins with such small steps.

The flow of power in a Christian society is from the inside-out. The flow of power in a pagan society is from the outside-in, from the top-down. This top-down flow occurs because the people see the rulers as the source of power and authority — they are the ultimate authority in the earth. However, the state is not man's savior nor the ultimate authority in the earth. Caesar thought he was, but Jesus made clear his authority was from God and was limited.[23] Most leaders throughout history have had this Caesar mentality, with most citizens agreeing. The spread of Christian ideas, especially after the Protestant Reformation, changed this in many nations, but, unfortunately, a majority of these nations are moving back toward a pagan view of government. Many people in the United States are embracing this idea as well. When trouble comes, who do people look to for help, provision, and "salvation"? Many first look to civil government, thinking the government owes them this provision. Many in the media agree, and often lambaste the government if it is not acting fast enough, being efficient, or providing enough relief. (Since it is not the purpose of civil government to provide all things for the citizens, it will never do this effectively or efficiently.)

Secularists have no savior, so they often look to government to be their savior — to bring peace, to establish a utopia, to meet needs, to provide material things, and so on. Christians have a Savior and do not need government for this. From a Christian perspective, civil government is a divine institution with a legitimate function, but it is very limited in what it is supposed to do. It is to protect the righteous, punish the evil doer, and administer God's justice in the civil realm that is under its sphere of authority.[24]

The Christian idea of government teaches that the state exists to serve man, not vice-versa; that government flows from the internal to the external, from the bottom-up; that government begins with self-government, then flows to the family, church, and the civil realm.

7. The Christian Idea of Education

The Christian idea of man teaches us that all men have great value, but that men are sinful, in a fallen state, and in need of a redeemer. We cannot save ourselves. We need the regenerating power of the Holy Spirit to work in us, to translate us into the kingdom of God. Once we become a new creation we must grow in our salvation — we must be sanctified in His truth so we can extend His kingdom in the nations. Biblical education is central in doing this.

All people must be educated so they can know the truth (God) themselves. In the fourth and fifth centuries, the church began to embrace a pagan philosophy of education, thinking only certain people can know and keep the truth (the Bible). These keepers of the truth (the clergy) would then tell the common person what that truth was. This practice led to bondage, as many people were cut off from the truth. The Protestant Reformation changed this. It brought forth the Christian idea of education; that is, everyone should know the truth themselves. Everyone should have access to the Bible, God's source of truth to mankind. This Christian idea motivated many people to translate the Bible into the common language of the people.

America's Founders were very much aware of the relation of education and liberty. They knew that a people cannot be ignorant and free. Jefferson said it this way: "If a nation expects to be ignorant and free, in a state of civilization, it expects what never was and never will be." Benjamin Franklin said that ignorance produces bondage: "A nation of well informed men who have been taught to know and prize the rights which God has given them cannot be enslaved. It is in the region of ignorance that tyranny begins."

Early Americans believed that useful education—that which produces liberty—must have its foundation in Christianity. To the Founders, Christianity was the source of liberty, all types of liberty. In the Preface to his *United States History* book, Noah Webster wrote:

> The brief exposition of the constitution of the United States, will unfold to young persons the principles of republican government; and it is the sincere desire of the writer that our citizens should early understand that the genuine source of correct republican principles is the Bible, particularly the New Testament or the Christian religion.[25]

Signer of the Declaration, Benjamin Rush wrote in 1806:

> Christianity is the only true and perfect religion, and that in proportion as mankind adopt its principles and obeys its precepts, they will be wise and happy.[26]

Education is much more than imparting knowledge and skills; it is preparing people to fulfill their destiny in assisting to advance God's Kingdom in the earth. G.K. Chesterton said: "Education is simply the soul of a society as it passes from one generation to another. Whatever the soul is like, it will have to be passed on somehow, consciously or unconsciously. . . . It is . . . the transfer of a way of life." Christian education passes on the Biblical way of life. State education today is passing on a secular, humanistic, socialistic way of life. Modern state education undermines liberty in two ways. One, it teaches a worldly philosophy that leads men into captivity (see Colossians 2:8). Two, it takes away from the family the role as primary educator.

The Bible teaches that parents have the right and responsibility to govern the education of their children. Embraced by early Americans, this idea motivated parents to educate their children at home, to start church and private schools, to found colleges, and to make education available to all citizens, including Native Americans. This produced a Biblically literate and educated nation. Everyone knew principles of liberty. Thus, these people could affect a Christian Revolution and give birth to the American Christian Constitutional Federal Republic.

Education in Biblical truth produced a free society with little crime. The crime that existed was a concern for the Founders, but they knew how to most effectively deal with it. Benjamin Rush wrote in 1806 that

> the only means of establishing and perpetuating our republican forms of government, . . . is, the universal education of our youth in the principles of christianity by the means of the bible. For this Divine book, above all others, favors that equality among mankind, that respect for just laws, and those sober and frugal virtues, which constitute the soul of republicanism.[27]

Education in colonial America was primarily centered in the home and church, with the Bible the focal point of all education. Schools were started to provide a Christian education to those who were not able to receive such training at home and to supplement home education. The first schools were private and started by the church. The first common or public schools (though not like public schools today) originated with the school laws of 1647 in Massachusetts, which stated, "It being one chief project of that old deluder, Satan, to keep men from the knowledge of the Scriptures."[28] America's Founders recognized that Satan wants to keep people ignorant. If he can keep them ignorant, he can keep them in bondage. This motivated them to not only start schools but also colleges.

Colleges and universities were started as seminaries to train a godly and literate clergy. In fact, 106 of the first 108 colleges were founded on the Christian faith. One of the original rules and precepts of Harvard College stated:

> Let every Student be plainly instructed, and earnestly pressed to consider well, the end of his life and studies is, to know God and Jesus Christ which is eternall life, (John 17:3), and therefore to

lay Christ in the bottome, as the only foundation of all sound knowledge and Learning.[29]

The Father of the American Revolution, Samuel Adams, declared that education in the principles of the Christian religion is the means of renovating our age. He wrote in a letter October 4, 1790, to John Adams, then vice-president of the United States:

> Let divines and philosophers, statesmen and patriots, unite their endeavors to renovate the age, by impressing the minds of men with the importance of educating their little boys and girls, of inculcating in the minds of youth the fear and love of the Deity and universal philanthropy, and, in subordination to these great principles, the love of their country; of instructing them in the art of self-government, without which they never can act a wise part in the government of societies, great or small; in short, of leading them in the study and practice of the exalted virtues of the Christian system.[30]

Knowledge apart from God and His truth is little better than complete ignorance, because the most important aspect of education is the imbuing of moral principles. All education is religious — it imparts a basic set of principles and ideals, a worldview. How the youth are educated today will determine the course the nation takes in the future.

According to Adams, the key to renovating America today is to instruct our youth in the study and practice of Christianity, of imparting to citizens the seven Christian ideas upon which the nation was built. Americans must be given the truth, including the truth of our history and founding principles.

A seed form of the seven ideas that made America successful was planted in all of the original colonies. Some of these ideas were more fully embraced by some of the colonists than others, and there was certainly a need for these ideas to grow and produce fruit, which is what occurred during the one and a-half centuries from Jamestown to independence. Unfortunately, the story of the

Christian source of America's liberties and founding ideas is not being told today. As 2007 marks the 400th anniversary of the founding of Virginia, and hence America, it is appropriate to tell some of the story of those who were influential in the beginning of the first permanent English settlement in America. We will start with the story of the first Founding Father of America.

Chapter 3

Vision for Planting — Richard Hakluyt and the Providential Colonization of America

"Wee shall by plantinge [in America] inlarge the glory of the gospell... and provide a safe and a sure place to receave people from all partes of the worlds that are forced to flee for the truthe of Gods worde."

Richard Hakluyt, 1584

No man was more influential in the establishment of the American colonies than Richard Hakluyt. This minister, who from Biblical inspiration became the greatest English geographer of the Elizabethan epoch, compiled the records of numerous European explorations, voyages, and settlements with the view of encouraging England to establish colonies in the New World. True to the calling God had put into his heart, the spreading of the gospel and establishment of the Christian faith in new lands was at the forefront of his motives in undertaking this great task. Hakluyt also foresaw America as a land where persecuted Christians could find refuge.

Historian William Robertson wrote that England was "more indebted" to Richard Hakluyt for her American colonies "than to any man of that age."[1] J.A. Williamson wrote: "The history of Elizabethan expansion is to a great extent the work of Richard Hakluyt, to a greater extent perhaps than the record of any other large movement can be ascribed to the labors of any one historian. He preserved a mass of material that would otherwise have perished, and he handled it with an enthusiasm and common sense which have made his work live through the centuries."[2] "As author, editor, and propagandist [Richard Hakluyt] did more than any other man or score of men to waken Englishmen to what he was assured was their true destiny."[3]

In Hakluyt's first writings, *Divers Voyages Touching the Discovery of America*, published in 1582, he lamented that while Spain and Portugal had planted colonies in the new world, England had not "the grace to set fast footing on such fertill and temperate places as are left as yet unpossessed."[4] And as he clearly revealed, England had the right to colonize these unpossessed lands due to the discovery of them by John Cabot in 1497.

In 1584 Hakluyt presented his *Discourse on Western Planting* to Queen Elizabeth where he set forth the principal reasons for colonization. First and foremost was the religious reason. He said that colonization would make for "the enlargement of the gospel of Christ."[5] He saw that propagating the gospel would include the conversion and civilization of the Indians. "Hakluyt lamented that he had not heard of a single *infidel* converted by the English explorers."[6]

In Chapter 20 of the *Discourse*, Hakluyt states numerous reasons for planting new colonies including: "Wee shall by plantinge there inlarge the glory of the gospell, and from England plante sincere relligion, and provide a safe and a sure place to receave people from all partes of the worlds that are forced to flee for the truthe of Gods worde."[7] Many of the early settlers of America reiterated this idea. Hakluyt was the first to proclaim the providential purposes of America.

Matthew Page Andrews wrote that "Hakluyt fired the vital spark of religious purpose that played a compelling part in American colonization when England was swayed by the strong convictions of the Protestant political and religious revolution culminating in the Puritan upheaval."[8]

"Richard Hakluyt was not simply a historian and a collector: he was also an agitator and a prophet."[9] He imparted the vision for and directed the colonization of the greatest and most free nation in history.

Early Life and Inspiration for God's Calling

Richard Hakluyt, Preacher, (as he described himself to distinguish him from his cousin of the same name) was born about 1552 in or near London. His father and mother both died in 1557, so he was orphaned at about age five. His cousin Richard (the lawyer) agreed to look after his relative of the same name. In 1564 (the year Shakespeare was born) he entered Westminster School, where he studied for about 6 years, proving to be a diligent scholar. In 1568, while Hakluyt was at Westminster, he visited his cousin one day in the Middle Temple. This meeting providentially provided the impulse which determined his lifework. In the preface to the first edition of his *Principal Navigations* (1589), Hakluyt records his story.

> I do remember that being a youth, and one of her Majesty's scholars at Westminster, that fruitful nursery, it was my hap to visit the chamber of Master Richard Hakluyt, my cousin, a gentleman of the Middle Temple, at a time when I found lying open upon his board certain books of cosmography with a universal map. He, seeing me somewhat curious in the view thereof, began to instruct my ignorance by showing me the division of the earth into three parts after the old account, and then according to the later and better distribution into more. He pointed with his wand to all the known seas, gulfs, bays, straits, capes, rivers, empires, kingdoms, dukedoms, and territories of each part, with declaration also of their special commodities and particular wants, which by benefit of traffic and intercourse of merchants are plentifully supplied. From the map he brought me

to the Bible, and turning to Psalm 107 directed me to the twenty-third and twenty-fourth verses, where I read that they which go down to the sea in ships and occupy by the great waters, they see the works of the Lord and His wonders in the deep, etc. Which words of the Prophet together with my cousin's discourse (things of high and rare delight to my young nature) took in me so deep an impression that I constantly resolved if ever I were preferred to the University, where better time and more convenient place might be ministered for these studies, I would by God's assistance prosecute that knowledge and kind of literature, the doors whereof (after a sort) were so happily opened before me.[10]

"This incident gives the key-note of his life. He presently did go to the university, becoming in 1570 a student at Christ Church, Oxford; and he did his regular work there faithfully and in due course took his degree; but every spare moment he devoted to his favorite field."[11] Hakluyt wrote:

I fell to my intended course and by degrees read over whatsoever printed or written discoveries and voyages I found extant either in the Greek, Latin, Italian, Spanish, Portugal, French, or English languages; and in my public lectures was the first that produced and showed both the old imperfectly composed and the new lately reformed maps, globes, spheres, and other instruments of this art for demonstration in the common schools, to the singular pleasure and general contentment of my auditory.[12]

In 1578 Hakluyt was ordained a priest in the Church of England. He held a professorship of divinity, served as chaplain to the English Embassy at Paris, received a patent from Sir Walter Raleigh to discover new lands, served as prebend in the cathedral of Bristol and rector of Wetheringsett in Suffolk, and finally became prebendary and then archdeacon of Westminster. He was married twice, had one son, and lived a comfortable life, being respected by the Queen and her ministers. He died in 1616 in his mid-sixties and was buried in Westminster Abbey, but no inscription marks his grave. "Through all these years he devoted himself unremittingly to the purpose formed as a boy in his visit to the Middle Temple."[13]

Hakluyt's Character and Influence

Richard Hakluyt was a mild, scholarly preacher who knew more about the New World than any man; yet, he never saw it. "He helped give form to the British Empire when it was little more than a dream" "Virtually every ship that came to the colonies in the seventeenth century carried a set of the Voyages," or at least that volume that dealt with the New World, with the purpose of guiding and acclimating them there. John Smith included much of Hakluyt's writings in his *General History* and William Bradford mentions Hakluyt in *Of Plymouth Plantation*; "both men sought to continue the story Hakluyt had begun."[14]

Hakluyt was a silent, modest man who was at ease with both wealthy statesmen and rowdy sailors. He had many prestigious friends but did not use these friendships for his own personal gain or recognition; rather, he employed their assistance to further the dream of colonization.

Hakluyt was indefatigable in research, traveling many places to talk with explorers and sailors, recording their first hand accounts; he gathered writings and accounts from many nations of voyages and travels; he searched out truth in many libraries. "He had a passion for truth, and once he rode 200 miles to check the facts about an early and insignificant expedition to America — Master Hore's in 1536 — from a lone survivor."[15] His contemporaries were most impressed by his enormous industry. He said that only a love of his country could induce him to undertake such exhausting labors. He wrote:

> I call the work a burden in consideration that these voyages lay so dispersed, scattered, and hidden in several hucksters' hands,

that I now wonder at myself to see how I was able to endure the delays, curiosity, and backwardness of many from whom I was to receive my originals. . . . What restless nights, what painful days, what heat, what cold I have endured; how many long and chargeable journeys I have travelled; how many famous libraries I have searched into; what variety of ancient and modern writers I have perused; what a number of old records, patents, privileges, letters, etc., I have redeemed from obscurity and perishing; into how manifold acquaintance I have entered; what expenses I have not spared; and yet what fair opportunities of private gain, preferment and ease I have neglected.[16]

"His life is a notable example of how singleness of purpose and dogged persistence, in a man not endowed, so far as we can tell, with any of the more brilliant attributes of genius, lead him, as if inevitably, to high achievement and lasting fame."[17]

First Impetus for English Colonization of America

Hakluyt's first book was published in 1582 and was entitled: *Divers voyages touching the discovery of America and the islands adjacent to the same, made first of all by our Englishmen, and afterwards by the Frenchmen and Britons, &c.* This book was small enough and cheap enough to be bought by virtually anyone.

Divers Voyages is a pamphlet containing a collection of documents giving support for England's prior claim to possess and settle the coast of America. Its primary object was the

promotion of the colonization of America; and to enlighten his countrymen he brought together from all available sources the various accounts showing the history of the discovery of the east coast of North America, giving the fullest particulars then known, and giving the first impetus to the English colonization of America. "Virtually," says Sir Clements Markham, "Raleigh and Hakluyt were the founders of those colonies which eventually formed the United States. Americans revere the

name of Walter Raleigh; they should give an equal place to that
of Richard Hakluyt."[18]

In the preface to *Divers Voyages*, Hakluyt gives reasons for
colonization. He spoke of the desire of "reducing those gentile
people to Christianitie."[19] He also spoke of the desire to find
passage to Cathay (the Northwest Passage) so they could "make
the name of Christe to be known unto many idolaterous and
heathen people."[20]

He spoke of past attempts that had failed and then gave the
reason why he thought this occurred. He wrote that if past
attempts

> had not been led with a preposterous desire of seeking rather
> gaine than God's glorie, I assure myself that our labours had
> taken farre better effecte. But wee forgotte, that Godliness is
> great riches, and that if we first seeke the kingdome of God, al
> other thinges will be given unto us, and that as the light
> accompanieth the Sunne and the heate the fire, so lasting riches
> do wait upon them that are jealous for the advancement of the
> Kingdome of Christ, and the enlargement of his glorious
> Gospell: as it is sayd, I will honour them that honour mee. I trust
> that now being taught by their manifold losses, our men will
> take a more godly course, and use some part of their goodes to
> his glory: if not, he will turne even ther covetousnes to serve
> him, as he hath done the pride and avarice of the Spaniards &
> Portingales, who pretending in glorious words that they made
> ther discoveries chiefly to convert infidelles to our most holy
> faith (as they say) in deed and truth sought not them, but their
> goods and riches.[21]

To accomplish these and other goals, Richard Hakluyt
suggested increasing the training and knowledge of seamen.
Throughout his life he encouraged some sort of faculty or school
to be established to train men in all areas necessary to become a

complete navigator. Such a school was not realized for a number of centuries.

Hakluyt Providentially Saved from Fateful Voyage

Hakluyt's *Divers Voyages* brought him directly into the circle of people who were seeking to explore North America. He became an advisor and supporter to many, including Sir Humphrey Gilbert. When Gilbert was planning his 1583 expedition, Hakluyt arranged for an educated observer to accompany him for the purpose of collecting information. Hakluyt intended to fill this role, but just prior to the voyage he was appointed as chaplain to Sir Edward Stafford, Queen Elizabeth's ambassador in Paris, so he traveled to France, where he would remain for five years. He arranged for Stephen Parmenius to go instead. So in June 1583 when Gilbert's expedition set sail, Parmenius was on the flagship and not Hakluyt. His appointment in France saved his life, for during the expedition the ship that carried Gilbert and Parmenius, the *Squirrel*, went down at sea because of great storms.

Though he providentially went to France instead of sailing to North America, his intentions of promoting English colonization did not change. In France he wrote "A Particular Discourse concerning Western Discoveries" (though it was not printed at this time). In this work, Hakluyt reiterates the case that England had claim to North America by virtue of discovery by the Cabots in 1497. He urged England to follow Spain's lead in colonizing the New World.

Discourse of Western Planting, 1584

In the autumn of 1584, while visiting London, Hakluyt presented this original work to Queen Elizabeth. It had been drafted at the request of Sir Walter Raleigh, who had chosen Hakluyt as a spokesman to promote his plans to the Queen. It contained 21 chapters stating the case for discovery and colonization. The first chapter was entitled: "That this westerne discoverie will be greately for thinlargemente of the gospell of Christe, whereunto the Princes of the refourmed Relligion are Chefely bounde, amongeste whome her Matie ys principall."[22]

In this chapter he explained with notes from explorers how the inhabitants of the new lands were not Christian but worshiped false gods. He said it was their chief duty as a nation to convert these people and enlarge "the glorious gospell of Christe." He quoted Paul in Romans 10 of the necessity of sending preachers so people could hear the word and be converted. As "defenders of the faith," Hakluyt wrote, the Kings and Queens of England "are not onely chardged to mayneteyne and patronize the faithe of Christe, but also to inlarge and advance the same: Neither oughte this to be their laste worke but rather the principall and chefe of all others, accordinge to the comoundemente of our Saviour Christe."[23]

Hakluyt then quotes Matthew 6:33 to seek first the Kingdom of God. He said the way for the English to accomplish this would be to establish one or two colonies near the natives in the new world. This would enable them to learn the natives' language and manners while in safety "and so wth discrecion and myldenes distill into their purged myndes the swete and lively liquor of the gospell."[24]

He said that the attempts at colonization by the Portuguese and Spanish had only minimal success because they lacked the purity of true religion. With true religion, they could do better. Hakluyt then speaks of the Macedonian call that Paul received in Acts 16 and that God providentially moved to get Paul to go where God intended. Hakluyt then related how God had similarly frustrated the English from going other ways and how He sent out a "Macedonian" call from America: "the people of America crye oute unto us their nexte neighboures to come and helpe them, and bringe unto them the gladd tidinges of the gospell."[25] Hakluyt goes on to say that God would provide the funds necessary to carry on this great work and He would bless those who support it. The chronicler then encourages Queen Elizabeth to get behind this endeavor and be a part of converting many infidels to Christ.

To Hakluyt, mission work was of primary importance, and to do this effectively, thriving colonies needed to be established.

Chapter 20 of the *Discourse* contains a brief collection of reasons to induce the Queen and the state to undertake the western voyage and planting. In one of these Hakluyt says: "Wee shall by plantinge there inlarge the glory of the gospell, and from England plante sincere relligion, and provide a safe and a sure place to receave people from all partes of the worlde that are forced to flee for the truthe of Gods worde."[26]

A few copies of Hakluyt's *Discourse* were made at this time, but it essentially remained hidden for three centuries until it was printed in 1877 in the state of Maine, one of the regions Hakluyt wished to colonize. Since it was not available to later generations it has not received the recognition it deserves as giving an "indispensable record of the motives and intentions of the first colonizers."[27] Here "are the blueprints for the British Empire in America from 1606 to 1776."[28]

The Queen accepted his ideas but did not initiate state-sponsored colonizations because relations with Spain were too tense. This and the war with Spain a few years later put off a national effort at colonization for some decades. Raleigh, though, did pursue his own efforts at establishing a colony in the New World. His attempt at Roanoke, which began in 1585, failed.[29]

Hakluyt returned to France and while there he made a discovery "which must have been very galling to him. He found everybody discussing the great voyages of discovery made by the Spanish, Portuguese and Italians, while his own countrymen were looked upon as idle stay-at-homes. Immediately upon his return to England he determined to correct this impression, which was a very false one, and he commenced to place on record the various enterprises upon which the English had been engaged. The result of his labours was the first edition of *The Principal Navigations, Voyages, Traffiques and Discoveries of the English Nation.*[30]

His trip to France not only averted his potential death on Gilbert's voyage, but also enabled him to gather information on French, Portuguese, and Spanish voyages.

Principal Navigations

Throughout his life, Hakluyt collected, compiled, and edited voyages to the new world, telling the story with the view of encouraging colonization. He gave numerous reasons why England should colonize the New World. The first and foremost in his mind was for religious reasons (as has been mentioned), which was consistent with the life of this man of piety. A second reason was political — colonies in the New World would act as a bridle to keep the King of Spain from gaining too much power. The third was economic — new colonies would provide a means of increasing wealth via trade and would promote industrialization, both of which would help to end unemployment in England. Hakluyt had a great concern for the poor in his native country and he saw new colonies as a means to assist them in overcoming poverty.[31]

Hakluyt returned to England from France in 1588. The next year he published in one volume the first edition of his most famous work, *The Principal Navigations, Voyages, and Discoveries of the English Nation.* An enlarged three-volume edition was published 1598-1600. The first and second volume dealt with the Old World, the third with the New. The one-volume, first edition ends with an account of the vanquishing of the Spanish Armada, or, as Hakluyt entitled it, "The Miraculous Victory Atchieved by the English Fleete," and it was quite miraculous.

In 1588, Philip II of Spain sent the Spanish Armada to bring England and the Low Countries (the Netherlands) again under the domination of the Holy Roman Empire. One-half century before, under Henry VIII, England had split from Rome and established her own church, the Church of England. Holland had also separated from Catholic control and had already been engaged with the Spanish in many battles. Those faithful to Rome had not appreciated the direction these two countries were taking and had sought for ways to bring them back into the fold of the Catholic religion. With the rise of Puritanism and Separatism in England and Holland, these renegades were straying even further from the established religion. With the build-up of the massive Spanish fleet, there was now a way to bring these nations back to the true faith. King Philip had amassed a mighty navy "as never the like had before that time sailed upon the Ocean sea."[32] It was comprised of 134 ships and about 30,000 men; Spain considered it invincible.

When the English learned that the Armada was being assembled to be sent against them, they began to prepare as best as they could, but they had many fewer ships that were smaller and not nearly as well armed. Their only hope was for a miracle to occur. People gathered throughout England to pray for such a miracle — especially those of the reformed faith because the Spanish specifically mentioned them as a target of their attack, for they knew these reformers were the major threat to the re-establishment of the Catholic religion in England. Richard Hakluyt records:

> [I]t is most apparant, that God miraculously preserved the English nation. For the L. Admirall wrote unto her Majestie that in all humane reason, and according to the judgement of all men (every circumstance being duly considered) the English men were not of any such force, whereby they might, without a miracle, dare once to approch within sight of the Spanish Fleet: insomuch that they freely ascribed all the honour of their victory

unto God, who had confounded the enemy, and had brought his counsels to none effect.

While this woonderfull and puissant Navie was sayling along the English coastes, and all men did now plainely see and heare that which before they would not be perswaded of, all people thorowout England prostrated themselves with humble prayers and supplications unto God: but especially the outlandish Churches (who had greatest cause to feare, and against whom by name, the Spaniards had threatened most grievous torments) enjoyned to their people continuall fastings and supplications, that they might turne away Gods wrath and fury now imminent upon them for their sinnes: knowing right well, that prayer was the onely refuge against all enemies, calamities, and necessities, and that it was the onely solace and reliefe for mankinde, being visited with affliction and misery. Likewise such solemne dayes of supplication were observed thorowout the united Provinces.

As the Spanish fleet sailed up the English Channel, they were met by the much smaller English and Dutch navies. In the natural, the English had little hope, yet England and Holland had been fasting and praying. A series of storms caused many of the Armada ships to sink, disease wiped out many of the Spanish troops, and other providential occurrences resulted in a resounding defeat of the invincible Armada. Of the original force only 53 ships returned to Spain with less than half of the original 30,000 men. It seemed apparent to those delivered that "God . . . fought for them in many places with his owne arme."

After this miraculous defeat, Holland minted coins as a perpetual memory. Of one coin Hakluyt recorded: "on the one side contained the armes of Zeland, with this inscription: GLORY TO GOD ONELY: and on the other side, the pictures of certeine great ships, with these words: THE SPANISH FLEET: and in the circumference about the ships: IT CAME, WENT, AND WAS. Anno 1588. That is to say, the Spanish fleet came, went, and was vanquished this yere; for which, glory be given to God onely."

They minted another coin that "upon the one side whereof was represented a ship fleeing, and a ship sincking: on the other side foure men making prayers and giving thanks unto God upon their knees; with this sentence: Man purposeth; God disposeth. 1588."

England and Holland marked the victory with public days of fasting and prayer. Hakluyt writes:

> Also a while after the Spanish Fleet was departed, there was in England, by the commandement of her Majestie [Elizabeth], and in the united Provinces, by the direction of the States, a solemne festivall day publikely appointed, wherein all persons were enjoyned to resort unto the Church, and there to render thanks and praises unto God: and the Preachers were commanded to exhort the people thereunto. The foresayd solemnity was observed upon the 29 of November; which day was wholly spent in fasting, prayer, and giving of thanks.

The Queen rode into London in great triumph and fanfare and all the people turned out with banners and ensigns heralding the event.

> Her Majestie being entered into the Church, together with her Clergie and Nobles gave thanks unto God, and caused a publike Sermon to be preached before her at Pauls crosse; wherein none other argument was handled, but that praise, honour, and glory might be rendered unto God, and that Gods name might be extolled by thanksgiving.[33]

Charter for Colonization

When King James I came to the throne in 1603, the English militant foes of Spain were curbed and peace was established with Spain. As a result, Raleigh was imprisoned in 1605 and he lost his rights to lands in America. On April 10, 1606, a charter was issued to Gates, Somers, Hakluyt, Wingfield, Hanham, and others who established the London and Plymouth Companies.

The incorporators of this charter were resolved into two groups. One was the London Company, usually called the Virginia Company, and was entitled to establish the first colony between 34 and 38 degrees north latitude; the other was the Plymouth Company which was to establish the "second colony," between 41 and 44 degrees north latitude. The area in between was to be open to both companies.

King James gave them authority to plant colonies in that part of America called Virginia and other parts "which are not now actually possessed by any Christian Prince or People." The reason for their endeavors was stated as:

> We, greatly commending, and graciously accepting of, their Desires for the Furtherance of so noble a Work, which may, by the Providence of Almighty God, hereafter tend to the Glory of his Divine Majesty, in propagating of Christian Religion to such People, as yet live in Darkness and miserable Ignorance of the true Knowledge and Worship of God, and may in time bring the Infidels and Savages, living in those parts, to human Civility, and to a settled and quiet Government: DO, by these our Letters Patents, graciously accept of, and agree to, their humble and well-intended Desires.[34]

This charter extended the rights of Englishmen to any new colonies that would be established.

In 1606, Hakluyt was named one of the four London patentees in the first Virginia Company charter. On November 24, 1606, Hakluyt was granted dispensation to hold a living in Jamestown without relinquishing his English preferments. This meant he could go to Jamestown as the officially recognized clergyman, to be paid like parish preachers in England, and he would not have to give up the church offices he held in England. The grant Hakluyt received from the King mentions that Hakluyt and Robert Hunt, along with other men, had the authority to start a colony in America. To Hakluyt and Hunt it was written: "And that you may the more freely and better watch and perform the ministry and preaching of God's word in those parts," they could leave their charges in England and still take payment for them.[35]

So Hakluyt was named on the first company patent for the Virginia colony, was part of the first directorate, and was probably intended to be the head of the church in the colony. He would have gone with the first colonists to Virginia in 1607 but age or infirmity prevented him. Hakluyt recommended that Hunt go in his place.[36]

Attempts to Stop English Colonization

On June 25, 1605, a treaty of peace between Spain and England was signed by Philip III which opened the way for the English to settle in North America, though such colonization was opposed by many Spanish diplomats. When Pedro de Zuniga, the Spanish Ambassador to England, learned that plans had begun to establish a colony, he wrote to Philip giving him warning.

Pedro de Zuniga was the Spanish Ambassador to England, but also acted as a spy. He was very much opposed to English colonization in the New World and did all he could to stop it, but God providentially prohibited his efforts.

When Zuniga learned of the London Company's plans in 1606, he tried to visit King James I and exert pressure on him to stop the expedition, but Zuniga was laid flat on his back and could not get out of bed. He wrote: "It pleased God that since that day I have not been able to rise from my bed."[37]

Zuniga recovered and attempted to meet with the King with the intention of threatening war with Spain if the plans continued to start a new colony. Such a threat would have influence for Spain greatly outnumbered England in ships and arms (though Spain's complete dominance of the seas had subsided after the defeat of the Armada in 1588). Zuniga knew James would do all he could to keep England out of war with Spain and he believed he could pressure James to put a stop to colonization, even though colonization was being carried out by private enterprise.

An appointment was scheduled, but on the set day, James had a fever and could not see Zuniga. He put off other meetings because of grief over the death of his little daughter, Mary, and due to certain internal and external difficulties that arose. Had this last minute attempt by Zuniga been successful, it is likely the Spanish Ambassador could have pressured James to stop the expedition. By the time Zuniga was able to meet James, the colonists had set sail, departing on December 20, 1606. (The departure date was kept secret because, despite the recent declaration of peace between England and Spain, there were fears the fleet might be intercepted by the Spanish who opposed English colonization.) James was able to deflect Zuniga's threats claiming he had nothing to do with the Company's attempt at colonization – it was a private adventure, he said. James told Zuniga "that those who went, went at their own risk, and if they were caught there, there could be no complaint if they were punished."[38] James allowed future supply ships to sail to Virginia; however, the threats did so worry the King that, by summer's end in 1607, he pulled away his attention from the new colony.

After Jamestown was established, Zuniga continued in his efforts to see it crushed. He wrote to King Philip and urged him "to command that the English in Virginia should be destroyed with the utmost possible promptness." And not just once, but he wrote his king repeatedly, urging him in every way "to give orders to have the insolent people [in Virginia] quickly annihilated."[39] On October 8, 1607, Zuniga wrote the king that he thought "it very desirable that an end should be now made of the few who are there, as that would be digging up the Root, so that it could put out no more." On October 16 he advised the king: "It will be serving God and your Majesty to drive these villains out from there, hanging them in time which is short enough for the purpose."[40]

And again, on December 6, Zuniga reports to Philip: "As to Virginia, I hear that three or four other ships will return there. Will your Majesty give orders that measures be taken in time; because now it will be very easy, and quite difficult afterwards, when they have taken root, and if they are punished in the beginning, the result will be that no more will go there."[41]

On March 28, 1608, Zuniga wrote the king telling him of plans by the London Council to send hundreds of men to Jamestown, and that he thought Philip should have them intercepted on the way. Ever zealous, Zuniga wrote again on November 8: "It is very important, Your Majesty should command that an end be put to those things done in Virginia; because it is a matter of great importance — and they propose (as I understand) to send as many as 1500 men there; and they hope that 12,000 will be gotten together there in time."[42]

The slow response of the Spanish king, with God's Providence displayed in many other ways, all worked together to assure the successful planting of the first permanent English settlement in America.

The First Colony

Orders and instructions given to the first colonists by the London Council emphasized the religious motive, as Hakluyt had been doing since his first writings in 1582. They wrote: "We do specially ordain, charge, and require" those concerned "with all diligence, care and respect" to provide that the "Christian faith be preached, planted, and used, not only within every of the said several colonies, and plantations, but also as much as they may arouse the savage people which do or shall adjoin unto them"; and that every one should "use all good means to draw the savages and heathen people . . . to the true service and knowledge of God."[43]

The instructions conclude: "Lastly and chiefly, the way to achieve good success, is to make yourselves all of one mind for the good of your country and your own, and to serve and fear God, the Giver of all Goodness; for every plantation which our Heavenly Father hath not planted shall be rooted out."[44]

Robert Hunt acted upon the desires of Hakluyt and the Council, faithfully conducting services in the New World and working to convert the Indians. (The Indian Navirans was probably his first convert and was of great assistance to the early Jamestown settlers.[45])

Hakluty's Legacy

Hakluyt died in 1616 at age sixty-four, leaving no portrait to show us his features nor monument to mark the great contributions of the man "who did more than any man of his generation to invigorate the efforts which eventually bore fruit in Virginia and New England."[46]

Richard Hakluyt is one of those heroes of Christian liberty of whom most Americans have never heard, yet, he is truly one of the Founding Fathers of this nation. We might even call him the first Founding Father, to whom God first gave the vision of America as the land of liberty, whose planting would "enlarge the glory of the gospel" and "provide a safe and a sure place to receive people from all parts of the worlds that are forced to flee for the truth of God's word." His Christian faith is revealed throughout his life, his writings, and in his death. In his last will and testament he wrote:

> First I commend my soule into the hands of God from whence I received the same, trusting thorow the only merits of Jesus Christ and the sanctification of the blessed Spirit to be

both in body and soule a member of His most holy and heavenly kingdome.[47]

Chapter 4

Planting the First Seeds — the Christian Influence in Jamestown and the Early Virginia Colony

Jamestown was the first permanent English settlement in the New World. Previous colonies were attempted in what would become the original United States, but none succeeded. Prior to the beginning of Jamestown in 1607, colonies were successfully planted in Canada and Central and South America, but in God's Providence the primary settlers of the American colonies were Englishmen and other Europeans who were products of the Protestant Reformation and who had a firm belief in God and the Bible. Their desire to establish a land of civil and religious freedom and to propagate the Gospel was evident in their lives, their laws, and their words.

We saw in the last chapter that Rev. Richard Hakluyt was instrumental in the colonization of Virginia and that his strong Christian faith was his central motive, as stated in his *Discourse on Western Planting*: "Wee shall by plantinge there inlarge the glory of the gospell, and from England plante sincere relligion, and provide a safe and a sure place to receave people from all partes of the worlds that are forced to flee for the truthe of Gods worde."[1] Hakluyt was the first to proclaim the Providential purposes of America. Many of the early settlers reiterated Hakluyt's view that this nation was to be a refuge for people desiring freedom. Symbolized much later by the Statue of

Liberty, this idea has been a key part of the American Dream from the beginning.

Charter for Christian Colonization

As previously stated, Richard Hakluyt and a number of other men were issued a charter on April 10, 1606, under which they established the London and Plymouth Companies for colonization in English America. King James gave this company of businessmen, missionaries, and explorers the authority to plant colonies in that part of America called Virginia and other parts "which are not now actually possessed by any Christian Prince or People." Their endeavor had multiple reasons, among which was clearly an evangelistic motive. This reason for their endeavors was stated in this first *Virginia Charter*:

> We, greatly commending, and graciously accepting of, their Desires for the Furtherance of so noble a Work, which may, by the Providence of Almighty God, hereafter tend to the Glory of his Divine Majesty, in propagating of Christian Religion to such People, as yet live in Darkness and miserable Ignorance of the true Knowledge and Worship of God, and may in time bring the Infidels and Savages, living in those parts, to human Civility, and to a settled and quiet Government: DO, by these our Letters Patents, graciously accept of, and agree to, their humble and well-intended Desires.[2]

The *Virginia Charter* not only committed America to a Christian purpose but also extended the rights of Englishmen to any new colonies that would be established. The London Council directing the company began to add details to their mission. On November 20, 1606, they issued *Articles, Instructions and Orders* in which was emphasized the religious motive for the colonists even more. They wrote: "We do specially ordain, charge, and require" those concerned "with all diligence, care and respect" to provide that the "Christian faith be preached, planted, and used, not only within every of the said several colonies, and plantations, but also as much as they may arouse the savage people which do or shall adjoin unto them"; and that every one should "use all good means to draw the savages and heathen people . . . to the true service and knowledge of God."[3]

The *Instructions of the London Virginia Company* added in 1606 that: "Lastly and chiefly the way to prosper and achieve good success is to . . . serve and fear God the Giver of all Goodness, for every plantation which our Heavenly Father has not planted shall be rooted out."[4] These words were inscribed on a monument in 1907 at Jamestown Historical Park in honor of the 300th anniversary of the founding of Jamestown. They provide today's visitor to this site proof, from an original source, of the Christian motivation behind the beginning of America. According to another statement published by the Virginia Company, entitled *A True and Sincere Declaration*, the "principal and main ends," of the settlers,

> were first to preach and baptize into the Christian religion, and by propagation of the Gospel, to recover out of the arms of the Devil, a number of poor and miserable souls, wrapt up unto death in almost invincible ignorance; to endeavor the fulfilling an accomplishment of the number of the elect which shall be gathered from all corners of the earth; and to add our mite to the treasury of Heaven.[5]

In the preface to John Smith's 1608 history of the colony, an unnamed author wrote of their purpose in the following manner:

> the end to the high glory of God, to the erecting of true religion among Infidells, . . . to the winning of many thousands of wandring sheepe, unto Christs fold, who now, and till now, have strayed in the unknowne paths of Paganisme, Idolatrie, and superstition: . . . whose Counsells, labours, godly and industrious endeavours, I beseech the mighty Jehovah to blesse,

prosper, and further, with his heavenly ayde, and holy assistance.[6]

Though some opposed the provision of propagating the Gospel to the natives, stating it would be their downfall, it proved to be their salvation and the key to their survival. The events that transpired show that without Hakluyt's insistence that ministers accompany the settlers, to not only perform their sacred duties for the English but also to seek to convert the Indians, Jamestown would not have survived and America could have had a different history.

In November, 1606, Hakluyt was named as the officially recognized clergyman for the new settlement and was probably intended to be the head of the church in the colony. As mentioned earlier, he was unable to accompany the first colonists so he recommended that Robert Hunt go in his place.[7]

Purpose of the Virginia Colony — "a business so full of piety."

Many people today say the primary, if not sole, purpose of those establishing Virginia was to make money as a business venture. An economic motive was surely present. It was a company that had to make money to endure. But when the original sources are consulted, the undeniable conclusion is that the people who took part in planting the Virginia colony consistently spoke of the Christian purpose, and many placed it foremost. Yet, modern historians repeatedly ignore or diminish the importance and relevance of this pious intention at Jamestown. The writings already mentioned, and those that follow, show that Virginia was much more than merely a business venture; it was, in the words of one early writer, "a business so full of piety."[8]

In 1607, George Percy was the first to write his *Observations gathered out of a Discourse of the Plantation of the Southerne*

Colonie in Virginia by the English. He became the fourth President of the Council that governed the colony. In his account he considered it important to mention that at their first landing on April 29th, "we set up a Cross at . . . Cape Henry."[9] Percy also spoke of the Providence of God in dealing with and using the Indians for their survival: "If it had not pleased God to have put a terror in the Savages hearts, we had all perished;"[10] and later, "It pleased God . . . to send those people which were our mortal enemies to relieve us with victuals."[11]

The first President of the Colony's Council was Edward Wingfield. In 1608 he wrote *A Discourse of Virginia* in which he also brings out the religious character of the colony. For instance, he writes that on June 22, 1607, "we made many prayers to our Almighty God." He described Captain Bartholomew Gosnold as being a "religious gent[leman]," and said that another captain, Christopher Newport, employed some of his men to build a church. He recognized that at key moments God's "mercy did now watch and ward for us" and "saved Mr. Smyth's life and mine." Describing their early government, of which Wingfield was a part, he wrote that to be sworn into office "the Council . . . took their oathes upon the Evangelists [i.e. the Gospels of the New Testament] to observe them," and he stated that his "first work" as president "was to make a right choice of a spiritual pastor."[12]

Pastor Hunt and the Colony's Early Religious Expression

One hundred and four colonists landed at Cape Henry on April 26, 1607. Three days later they erected a wooden cross near the shore where Rev. Robert Hunt led the men in prayer. Not long afterwards, they sailed across the bay and up a river that was named the James in honor of the king. On May 13, they reached the site they felt would be good for their settlement and called it Jamestown, also in honor of the king. Soon after going ashore,

Rev. Hunt "gathered his flock around him without delay, and standing in their midst under the trees uttered, for the first time in the western world, the solemn invocation: 'The Lord is in His Holy Temple; Let all the earth keep silence before Him.' The new land had been claimed for an earthly potentate; he now claimed it for the King of kings."

A triangular fort was built within a month after landing. The side facing the river was 420 feet in length, the other two sides were 300 feet long, and at each of the three corners bulwarks were built which contained 3 to 5 cannons. A sixty by twenty-four foot church would be built in the center of the fort, but until it was, services were held outdoors. Rev. Hunt preached from a wooden platform nailed between two trees and covered with a sail. In the words of John Smith, "For a Church we did hang an awning (which is an old sail) to three or foure trees to shadow us from the sunne. Our walls were rales of wood, our seats unhewed trees, till we cut plankes, our Pulpit a bar of wood nailed to two neighboring trees."[13]

It was here that the founder of the first Protestant church in America, Rev. Robert Hunt, conducted services until the church was built. This good and courageous clergyman preached twice each Sunday, read aloud the daily prayers, and celebrated communion once every three months. A special prayer was composed for the colonists that Hunt and others repeated each morning and evening at the King's command.

> Almighty God, . . . we beseech Thee to bless us and this plantation which we and our nation have begun in Thy fear and for Thy glory. . . . and seeing Lord, the highest end of our plantation here is to set up the standard and display the banner of Jesus Christ, even here where Satan's throne is, Lord let our labour be blessed in labouring for the conversion of the heathen. . . . Lord sanctify our spirits and give us holy hearts, that so we may be Thy instruments in this most glorious work.[14]

Morning and evening prayers were conducted for many years by the various ministers, civil leaders, or the captain of the watch. Part of the lengthy prayer presented at the changing of the guard in the fort stated:

> We know, O Lord, we have the Devil and all the gates of Hell against us, but if Thou, O Lord, be on our side, we care not who be against us. And, seeing by Thy motion and work in our hearts, we have left our warm rests at home and put our lives into Thy hands, principally to honor Thy name and advance the kingdom of Thy Son, Lord, give us leave to commit our lives into Thy hands.[15]

Rev. Hunt was not only the minister of Jamestown, but also one of the nine original Council members chosen by the Virginia Company to rule the Colony. He set the example of hard work for others, personally building the grist mill and taking care of the sick when at times there was only he and a handful to take care of all the rest. He preached against the proud and lazy and helped heal many divisions among the people. John Smith marveled at "that honest, religious, courageous divine," who in his service at Jamestown lost "all but the clothes on his back, [but] none did ever hear him repine his loss."[16]

Rev. Hunt fulfilled the desires of the London Council by not only conducting services in the New World, but also by working to convert the Indians. His first convert was an Indian named Navirans, who was very helpful to the early colonists.[17] Unfortunately, Hunt died in July of 1608. John Smith wrote that "till he could not speak, he never ceased to his utmost to animate us constantly to persist; whose soul, questionless, is with God."[18] On his memorial, which can be seen today at Jamestown, is written a fitting epitaph for the first Protestant minister to lose his life in order for the gospel to come to the New World:

> He preferred the service of God to every thought of ease at home. He endured every privation, yet none ever heard him

repine. . . . He planted the first Protestant church in America, and
laid down his life in the foundation of Virginia.

Captain John Smith

The colonists were careful in selecting a site to settle and felt
they had chosen a good location at Jamestown. At this spot the
river was deep enough for ships to anchor right next to the land,
and they felt it would be easy to defend themselves from an Indian
attack by land or a Spanish attack by sea. Yet, they would learn
later that the swamps that surrounded Jamestown were full of
mosquitoes that could cause malaria. Also, some of the water they
drank in that area was impure and would later cause typhoid fever
and dysentery.

The first year at Jamestown was a time of crisis due to
sickness, lack of food, and lack of strong leadership. In their
second year, Captain John Smith was chosen as the second
President of the Virginia Council. This explorer, soldier, and
author provided the strong leadership needed for survival. Smith
is called the "Father of Virginia" due to his significant
contributions in the establishment and survival of Jamestown.
After he was chosen as leader in September, 1608, one of the
things that he required of everyone was to go to church. Rev. Hunt
had died in July of that year and the church had fallen into
disrepair. Smith had it restored and said that "we had daily
common prayer . . . and surely God did most mercifully hear
us."[19]

When threatened, he fought the Indians, yet also made the
breakthroughs in peaceful relations with them that were essential
for survival. His courage, honesty, good sense, and skill as the
colony's second president set an example that the colonists
needed, and his insistence that everyone work hard was an
essential ingredient for their survival. Since the Jamestown
colonists were not a covenanted group of people from one church
congregation (as were the majority of the Pilgrims of Plymouth in

1620), unity was very difficult. At first they lacked the character and unselfishness to put work before adventure and material gain. As a result, they almost starved to death. But Smith made a rule based on the Bible: "he that will not worke shall not eat."[20] He refused lodging for himself until all others had it first. Due to an injury in 1609, Smith had to return to England, but his one year of leadership made the difference. (John Smith later also contributed to the success of the Pilgrims in Plymouth by carrying Squanto back to his home on a voyage Smith made from England to New England in 1619. Two years later Squanto providentially helped the Pilgrims to survive.)

Smith made a detailed map of Virginia and wrote an early history called *A True Relation* (1608) in which he refers to their practice of erecting crosses. On May 24, while exploring the James River, he stopped at the site of the future town of Richmond, saying that, "there we erected a cross."[21] Crosses were placed on his map at this spot, at Cape Henry (which was the location where they planted a cross on April 29, 1607), and also at many other locations. It is possible that actual crosses were erected at each spot where crosses exist on his map.[22]

Smith, like President Percy, often credited their survival to God's direct assistance. Following are a few more examples of Smith's references to God:

- "God (beyond all their expectations), . . . caused them [the attacking Indians] to retire."
- "God (being angry with us) plagued us with such famine and sickness."
- "by God's assistance being well recovered; . . . it pleased God (in our extremity) to move the Indians to bring us Corn, ere it was half ripe, to refresh us, when we rather expected they would destroy us."
- "God (the absolute disposer of all hearts) altered their conceits."

- "Having thus by Gods assistance gotten good store of corn, notwithstanding some bad spirits not content with Gods providence, still grew mutinous."
- "the King of Paspahegh . . . took great delight in understanding . . . our God."
- "But in the midst of my miseries, it pleased God to send Captain Nuport."
- "The rest we brought well guarded, to Morning and Evening prayers."
- "In the afternoon, . . . we guarded them as before to the Church; and after prayer."
- "by Gods gracious assistance, . . . no doubt pleasing to almighty God."[23]

Smith and Pocahontas

When the settlers first arrived at Jamestown the Indians' initial reaction was fear, suspicion, and hostility. Two weeks after the English arrived, 200 Indians attacked the settlement killing two and wounding ten others. The hostile relationship with some of the natives would change, thanks in large part to a young daughter of Chief Powhatan. John Smith said that Pocahontas was "next under God . . . the instrument to preserve this colony from death, famine, and utter confusion."[24] She befriended the colonists from the beginning and led Smith to state that "God made Pocahontas."[25]

Smith wrote that, while exploring far up the Chickahominy River in December 1607, he was captured by a band of Indians and eventually taken to Powhatan's village. That Smith was taken to the village and not killed right away was quite providential. Other colonists that accompanied him on the trip were captured, tortured, and killed. Smith was held captive for weeks, during which time he diverted a surprise attack on the fort at Jamestown, and eventually procured his release. In his writings, Smith describes various events during his capture, including their "hellish" singing, yelling, and dancing.[26] Upon arrival at Powhatan's village, Smith was treated as a special guest and was given a big dinner. But in a short time he was ordered to be put to death. His head was placed on a large stone where Indians with clubs prepared "to beat out his braines," but at this moment Pocahontas took his "head in her armes and laid her owne upon his to save him from death."[27] She pleaded for his life, which her father granted.

Powhatan said they were now friends and Smith should go back to Jamestown, yet Smith was "still expecting (as he had done all this long time of his imprisonment) every houre to be put to one death or other: for all their feasting. But almightie God (by his divine providence) had mollified the hearts of those sterne Barbarians with compassion."[28] Thus, Smith attributed his salvation from death to God.

Pocahontas not only saved Smith, but also helped save the Jamestown settlers from death. During their first winter all their food ran out and Pocahontas was instrumental in getting the Indians to bring new supplies. One writer of that period said that "God the patron of all good indevours, in that desperate extremitie, so changed the hearts of the Salvages, that they brought such plenty of their fruits, and provision, as no man wanted."[29] She brought food to the starving colonists at other times as well, and also helped obtain peace treaties with the Indians. John Fiske writes of Pocahontas: "But for her friendly services on more than one occasion, the tiny settlement would probably have perished."[30]

Smith's personal faith is not only reflected in his many acknowledgments of God throughout his life, but is clearly stated in his Last Will and Testament of 1631: "First I commend my soule into the handes of Allmightie God my maker hoping through the merites of Christ Jesus my Redeemer to receave full remission of all my sinnes, and to inherit a place in the everlasting kingdome."[31]

"Starving Time," 1609-1610: Forging of Christian Character

The Christian motivation of the colony is seen also in a document written by one of the colonists in 1609 called *Nova Britannia*. In this tract there are multiple references to God including: "by Gods help," "God willing," "by Gods mercy," "by Gods blessing," "by Gods beginnings," "God assisting us," and others. More quotes from this document are found in the box on the next page, but following are a few highlights showing their purposes for their colony:

- "to advance and spread the kingdom of God, and the knowledge of the truth, among so many millions"
- "to advance the kingdom of God, by reducing savage people from their blind superstition to the light of Religion"
- "we seek nothing less then the cause of God."
- "We purpose to proclaim and make it known to them all. . . . First, in regard of God the Creator, and of Jesus Christ their Redeemer, if they will believe in him."[32]

While almost all of the early colonists in Virginia professed to be Christians, some, no doubt, were merely nominal Christians and poorly demonstrated what they professed. But many were certainly devout in their faith, like the author of *Nova Britannia*, and many displayed great Christian character, like Robert Hunt. Thus, a diverse group remained at Jamestown when Smith returned to England in 1609. George Percy became Governor in Smith's place until Lord Delaware arrived from England. Percy was a man of fine character but was not a decisive leader as Smith

Christian Faith in *Nova Britannia*, 1609[33]

- "The land which we have searched out is a very good land, if the Lord love us, he will bring our people to it, and will give it us for a possession."
- "their joy exceeded and with great admiration they praised God."
- "God may have the honor, and his kingdom advanced in the action done."
- "God that has said by Solomon: Cast thy bread upon the waters, and after many days thou shall find it: he will give the blessing."
- "in the truth of Religion, and . . . wholesome laws, under the mild government of Christian Kings"
- "God has reserved in this last age of the world, an infinite number of those lost and scattered sheep, to be won and recovered by our means."
- "in the sight of God, when our King shall come to make his triumph in heaven. The prophet Daniel does assure, that for this conquest of turning many unto righteousness, he shall shine as the stars for ever and ever."
- "Our Saviour Christ"
- "heavenly providence blessed his Navigations and public affairs"
- "The third sort to avoid, are evil affected Magistrates, a plague that God himself complains of by the Prophet Isaiah: O my people, they that lead thee, cause thee to err."
- "Whatsoever thy hand shall find to do, do it with all thy might."
- "by Divine providence"
- "a Christian State and true Religion."
- "the coming of Christ"

had been. When the Indians learned that Smith had left, they broke the peace and "did spoile and murther all they incountered."[34] Due to lack of discipline, lack of incentive, and weakness on Percy's part to enforce the laws of the colony, many people stopped working and recklessly ate up all the supplies. A new 1609 Charter would eventually create more incentive to work because it provided for private enterprise, but the communal farming system remained in place until 1611. Epidemics also broke out and many began to die. All of this brought much disorder. Houses and parts of the fort were torn down and used for fire wood. By this time Pocahontas had also been forbidden by Powhatan to communicate with or assist the colonists on penalty of death, so their greatest link with the Indians had been cut off.

As a result, the winter of 1609-10 became known as the "Starving Time." The settlers ate horses, snakes, cats, rats, roots and boiled leather and book covers to survive. One early historian wrote: "So great was our famine, that . . . one amongst the rest did kill his wife, powdered [salted] her, and had eaten part of her before it was knowne; for which hee was executed, as hee well deserved."[35] Of the 490 colonists in Jamestown in September 1609, only 59 were left alive six months later. The Memorial Cross that is at Jamestown Historical Park today marks the site where some 300 of them were hastily buried at night so that the Indians would not know how few were still alive. It is a fitting reminder of a Christian people that gave their lives to plant the seed of the American Dream.

In May of 1610, Sir Thomas Gates sailed into Jamestown with two ships which he, and other settlers heading for Jamestown, had built while shipwrecked in Bermuda. Gates was to be the interim governor until Lord Delaware's arrival a month later. While they had some supplies, there were not enough to last for very long. Therefore, the thin, half-naked, and desperate settlers decided to abandon Jamestown and return to England. Some of them wanted to burn what was left of Jamestown, but Gates, John Rolfe, and others stopped them. An early Virginia historian wrote: "God, who did not intend that this excellent country should be abandoned, put it into the heart of Sir T. Gates to save it."[36]

They boarded their boats and sailed to the mouth of the James River where they dropped anchor for the night. The next morning, as they continued their voyage, they met Lord Delaware who had come with three well-stocked ships from England. There were cries of joy from the colonists who thanked God that help had come in time. Mere minutes would have changed the whole course of the history of Jamestown, of Virginia, and perhaps of America. But at that precise moment, before one ship slipped out of the bay into the wide ocean, they were met with provisions and new colonists. It was one of the most providentially timed events in history; and since Jamestown had not been burned, they were able to return with renewed hope that the colony would succeed.

Lord Delaware, Christian Mission, and New Moral Laws

On Sunday, June 10, 1610, the colonists stood amid the remains of Jamestown as Lord Delaware stepped from his boat. "The new governor of Virginia knelt and prayed, thanking God that he had come in time to save the colony. He then led the settlers to the church where, at his request, a sermon of thanksgiving was preached,"[37] by the new Chaplain Rev. Richard Bucke (1573-1623) who had come with the fleet.

Lord Delaware was prepared and inspired to fulfill his role as the new supreme governor of the colony. Among other contributions, he abolished the communal farming system and gave each colonist his own plot of ground to cultivate. After receiving his appointment while in England, he had listened to the sermon delivered by the Reverend William Crashaw in honor of his obtaining the position.

> And thou most noble Lord, whom God hath stirred up to neglect the pleasures of England, and with Abraham to go from

thy country, and forsake thy kindred and thy father's house, to go to a land which God will show thee, give me leave to speak the truth. Thy ancestor many hundred years ago gained great honour to thy house but by this action thou augmenst it. . . . Remember, thou art a general of English men, nay a general of Christian men; therefore principally look to religion. You go to commend it to the Heathen, then practice it yourselves; make the name of Christ honourable, not hateful unto them.[38]

A history textbook formerly used in Virginia schools states:

Lord Delaware was a religious man, and he was determined that the colonists should have the opportunity to worship God. A bell was rung for prayers every day at ten in the morning and at four in the afternoon. All were required to attend church. Two sermons were preached on Sunday, and one on Thursday. The little church was decorated with flowers, and the colonists enjoyed the periods of peace and quiet spent there.[39]

The *Second Virginia Charter* of 1609 declared "that it shall be necessary for all such as inhabit within the precincts of Virginia to determine to live together in the fear and true worship of Almighty God, Christian peace, and civil quietness;" and that "the principal effect which we [the crown] can desire or expect of this action is the conversion and reduction of the people in those parts unto the true worship of God and the Christian religion." The second charter also made provision for "the true word of God and the Christian faith" to be "preached, planted and used, not only within the colonies, but as much as they may, amongst the Savage People."[40]

Before poor health forced him to return to England in March of 1611, Governor Delaware encouraged a diverse spiritual life in Virginia. Besides Richard Bucke, other clergymen were welcomed. A Puritan dissenter, Rev. William Mease, served from about 1609 to 1620. Two years later, in May 1611, a Presbyterian dissenter, Alexander Whitaker, arrived with the new governor,

Sir Thomas Dale. A friend and minister wrote of Whitaker's "resolution that God called him to Virginia:"

> He, without any persuasion but God and his own heart, did voluntarily leave his warm nest, and, to the wonder of his kindred and amazement of them that knew him, undertook this hard, but, in my judgment, heroical resolution to go to Virginia, and help to bear the name of God to the Gentiles. Men may muse at it, some may laugh, and others wonder at it; but well I know the reason. God will be glorified in his own works, and what he hath determined to do, he will find means to bring it to pass. For the perfecting of this blessed work he hath stirred up able and worthy men to undertake the manning and managing of it.[41]

Whitaker served as the pastor for the first two settlements started outside of Jamestown. New Bermuda and Henrico City were located many miles up the James River. Churches were built at both of these villages and Whitaker alternately resided at each of them. While there he taught doctrine sympathetic with Puritan ideas. Thus, these were the first settlements in the New World shaped by Puritan doctrine, existing many years before those in New England.

Many writings during this time reflect the strong Christian spirit in Virginia. Sir Walter Cope wrote in 1610: "The eyes of all Europe are looking upon our endeavors to spread the gospel among the heathen people of Virginia, to plant an English nation there and to settle a trade in those parts."[42] A pamphlet written in 1612, "The New Life of Virginia," states:

> This is the work that we first intended, and have published to the world, to be chief in our thoughts, to bring those Infidel people from the worship of Devils to the service of God. . . . Take their children and train them up with gentleness, teach them our English tongue and the principles of religion. Win the elder sort by wisdom and discretion; make them equal to you English in

case of protection, wealth, and habitation, doing justice on such as shall do them wrong.[43]

Ralph Hamor lived in Virginia for four years (1610-1614), and wrote *A True Discourse of the Present Estate of Virginia*, published in 1615. Hamor wrote that the work in Virginia would be for

> setling and finishing up a *Sanctum Sanctorum* an holy house, a Sanctuary to him, the God of the Spirits, of all flesh, amongst such poore and innocent seduced Savages . . . to lighten them that sit in darkenes, and in the shaddow of death, and to direct their feete in the waies of peace.[44]

In the preface it was asserted that

> when these poore Heathens shall be brought to entertaine the honour of the name, and glory of the Gospell of our blessed Saviour, when they shall testifie of the true and everliving God, and Jesus Christ to be their Salvation, their knowledge so inlarged and sanctified, that without him they confesse their eternal death: I do beleeve I say (and how can it be otherwise?) that they shall breake out and cry with rapture of so inexplicable mercie: Blessed be the King and Prince of England, and blessed be the English Nation, and blessed for ever be the most high God, possessor of Heaven and earth, that sent these English as Angels to bring such glad tidings amongst us.[45]

The *Discourse* described the Virginia Plantation as "a business so full of piety."[46] Hamor urged them to "proceede in a businesse so full of honour, and worth," even "if there were no secondary causes" (like business concerns) because "the already publisht ends, I meane the glory of God in the conversion of those Infidels, and the honour of our King and country"[47] were sufficient reasons in themselves. Thus, Hamor puts the pious motives as primary, and other things as secondary, just the opposite of many writers today. He concludes his *Discourse* reiterating this same idea.

> Now the Virginian plantation hath both these notable properties; . . . for what is more excellent, more precious and more glorious, then to convert a heathen Nation from worshipping the divell, to the saving knowledge, and true worship of God in Christ Jesus? what more praiseworthy and charitable, then to bring a savage people from barbarisme unto civilitie? . . . what more convenient then to have good seates abroad for our everflowing multitudes of people at home? what more profitable then to purchase great wealth, which most now adaies gape after over-greedily? All which benefits are assuredly to bee had and obtained, by well and plentifully upholding of the plantation in Virginia.[48]

He speaks of both a religious and business purpose in the Virginia colony, but he puts the intent of converting "a heathen nation" to God first. Not only that, he goes on to say that Christian men are needed to accomplish both purposes:

> And for the durableness of all these great and singular blessings, there can (by Gods assistance) be no doubt at all made, if mens hearts unto whom God hath lentabilitie) were but inlarged cheerefully to adventure and send good companies of honest industrious men thither with a mind to inlarge Christs kingdome: for then will God assuredly maintaine his owne cause.[49]

Hamor then concludes, saying that they will come to possess the land through love and that they will profit as they have freedom to labor and the blessing of God upon their work.[50]

Governor Dale, according to Rev. Whitaker, was "a man of great knowledge in Divinity, and of a good conscience in all his doings: both which Bee rare in a martial man."[51] Although a spiritual man, he imposed nearly totalitarian rule, which he felt necessary to see the colony survive. These extraordinary measures were for only a brief period of Jamestown's life, but they helped assure the lasting success of the new colony. Another important contribution of Dale's was his writing, along with Sir Thomas Gates and Sir Thomas West (Lord Delaware), "Laws Divine, Morall, and Martiall, etc." According to Professor David Flaherty, these laws, written between 1609 and 1612 "represented the first written manifestations of the common law in America."[52]

The Bible was clearly the source of their civil laws, and their Christian faith is evident throughout. Parts of the first six laws follow (more are listed in Appendix 1):

1. First since we owe our highest and supreme duty, our greatest and all our allegeance to him, from whom all power and authoritie is derived, . . . we must alone expect our successe from him, who is onely the blesser of all good attempts, the King of kings, the commaunder of commaunders, and Lord of Hostes, I do strictly commaund and charge all Captaines and Officers, . . . to have a care that the Almightie God bee duly and daily served, and that they call upon their people to heare Sermons, as that also they diligently frequent Morning and Evening praier themselves by their owne exemplar and daily life. . . .

2. That no man speake impiously or maliciously, against the holy and blessed Trinitie, or any of the three persons, that is to say, against God the Father, God the Son, and God the holy Ghost, or against the knowne Articles of the Christian faith, upon paine of death.

3. That no man blaspheme Gods holy name upon paine of death, or use unlawful oathes, taking the name of God in vaine, curse, or banne [an imprecation of a curse], upon paine of severe punishment. . . .

4. No man shall use any traiterous words against his Majesties Person, or royall authority upon paine of death.

5. No man shall speake any word, or do any act, which may tend to the derision, or despight [open defiance] of Gods holy word upon paine of death. . . .

> 6. Everie man and woman duly twice a day upon the first towling of the Bell shall upon the working daies repaire unto the Church, to hear divine Service. . . .[53]

Although these punishments to uphold religious practice seem harsh and unreasonable to the modern mind, they were not so for Europe at the time. Most people strongly believed that Christianity was the only source of liberty and justice. No nation could be free where people rejected God and His Word, thus, to them, the death penalty was considered appropriate for those promoting an overthrow of God and His founding principles. Undermining Christianity was the equivalent of treason since it meant the eventual overthrow of their society. It would be many years before the compulsion of belief and practice was considered no longer necessary.

Pastors, Pocahontas, and Christianization of the Native Americans

During his six years as a minister in Virginia (1611-1617), Rev. Alexander Whitaker not only served the English settlers but also the native Indians, and hence he is known as the "apostle to the Indians." He wrote a famous essay in 1613 entitled *Good News From Virginia* which influenced Europeans to colonize America for the glory of God. He asserted that the survival of Jamestown through those difficult years was proof "that the finger of God hath been the only true worker here; that God first showed us the place, God first called us hither, and here God by His special Providence hath maintained us."[54] Some excerpts from this pastor's pen are on the following page.

In 1613, during Dale's governorship, Pocahontas was treacherously sold by some Indians to an English sea captain, who took her to Jamestown as a hostage. Dale tried to trade her to her father, Chief Powhatan, for some English hostages he held, but he

Good News from Virginia, Alexander Whitaker[55]

- "let the beauty of the Lord our God be upon us; and direct thou the works of our hands upon us, even direct thou our handiworks."
- "if we consider the almost miraculous beginning, and continuance of this plantation, we must needs confess that God hath opened this passage unto us, and led us by the hand unto this work."
- "let the miserable condition of these naked slaves of the devil move you to compassion toward them. They acknowledge that there is a great good God, but know him not, having the eyes of their understanding as yet blinded: wherefore they serve the devil for fear, after a most base manner, sacrificing sometimes (as I have here heard) their own Children to him."
- "Awake you true-hearted English men, you servants of Jesus Christ, remember that the Plantation is God's and the reward your Country's. Wherefore, aim not at your present private gain, but let the glory of God, whose Kingdom you now plant, & good of your Country, whose wealth you seek, so far prevail with you, that you respect not a present return of gain for this year or two: but that you would more liberally supply for a little space, this your Christian work, which you so charitably began.
- "Wherefore you (right wise and noble Adventurers of Virginia) whose hearts God has stirred up to build him a Temple, to make Him a house, to conquer a Kingdom for Him here: be not discouraged with those many lamentable assaults that the devil has made against us: he now rages most, because he knows his kingdom is to have a short end. Go forward boldly, and remember that you fight under the banner of Jesus Christ, that you plant his Kingdom who has already broken the Serpent's head: God may defer his temporal reward for a season, but be assured that in the end you shall find riches and honor in this world, and blessed immortality in the world to come. And you my brethren my fellow laborers, send up your earnest prayers to God for his Church in Virginia, that since his harvest here is great, but the laborers few, he would thrust forth laborers into his harvest; and pray also for me that the ministration of his Gospel may be powerful and effectual by me to the salvation of many, and advancement of the kingdom of Jesus Christ to whom, with the Father and the holy Spirit, be all honor and glory forevermore, *Amen.*"

refused. Pocahontas was then placed in the care of Rev. Alexander Whitaker, who took her to his farm near Henrico.

During this period, Rev. Whitaker, Sir Thomas Dale, and Captain John Rolfe taught Pocahontas about Christianity and also taught her how to read. She memorized the Apostle's Creed, the Lord's Prayer, and the Ten Commandments, and she learned the answers to the questions of the short catechism. "In the spring of 1614, Whitaker reviewed her in the catechism, received her renunciation of paganism, heard her confession of faith in Jesus Christ,"[56] and baptized her from a font made from the trunk of a tree. She took the name Rebecca. In April of that year, at the age of about 17, she was married to Rolfe in the Jamestown Church at a service performed by Rev. Richard Bucke. Prior to the marriage, Rolfe had written to Governor Dale seeking his approval to marry her. Rofle's heart to obey and please God are the central theme throughout the letter. In one part he writes:

> Let therefore this my well advised protestation, which here I make between God and my own conscience, be a sufficient witness, at the dreadfull day of judgement (when the secret of all mens hearts shall be opened) to condemn me herein, if my chiefest intent and purpose be not, to strive with all my power of body and mind, in the undertaking of so mightie a matter, no way led (so farre forth as mans weaknesse may permit) with the unbridled desire of carnall affection: but for the good of this plantation, for the honour of our countrie, for the glory of God, for my owne salvation, and for the converting to the true knowledge of God and Jesus Christ, an unbelieving creature, namely Pokahuntas.[57]

In June of 1614, Thomas Dale wrote of Pocahontas' conversion and marriage:

> Powhatans daughter I caused to be carefully instructed in Christian Religion, who after shee had made some good progresse therein, renounced publickly her countrey Idolatry,

openly confessed her Christian faith, was, as she desired, baptised, and is since married to an English Gentleman of good understanding, (as by his letter unto me, countaining the reasons for his marriage of her you may perceive) another knot to binde this peace the stronger. Her Father, and friends gave approbation to it, and her uncle gave her to him in the Church: she lives civilly and lovingly with him, and I trust will increase in goodnesse, as the knowledge of God increaseth in her. She will goe into England with me, and were it but the gayning of this one soule, I will thinke my time, toile, and present stay well spent."[58]

Rev. Whitaker also wrote of these events around the same time: "one Pocahuntas or Matoa the daughter of Powhatan, is married to an honest and discreet English Gentleman Master Rolfe, and that after she had openly renounced her countrey Idolatry, confessed the faith of Jesus Christ, and was baptised; which thing Sir Thomas Dale had laboured along time to ground in her."[59]

In 1616 Pocahontas, John Rolfe, and their son, Thomas, traveled to England to visit. She died there in March, 1617, and was buried at St. George's Parish Church in Gravesend. John Smith later was said to have commented: "Poor little maid. I sorrowed much for her thus early death, and even now cannot think of it without grief, for I felt toward her as if she were mine own daughter."[60]

Thomas Rolfe would later return to America where he married an Englishwoman, Jane Poythress. "From their union descended seven successive generations of educators, ministers, statesmen, and lawmakers, among whom were the Blairs, the Bollings, the Lewises, and the Randolphs. One of Thomas' — and therefore Pocahontas' — most distinguished descendants was John Randolph of Roanoke, who represented Virginia in the United States House of Representatives and in the United States Senate. Thus, through her son and his descendants, Pocahontas lived on in American history."[61] This early Christian convert to the protestant faith is honored today at Jamestown with a statue located near the church.

First Representative Assembly Opens with Prayer, 1619

In 1612 Virginia was granted a new charter that gave the Virginia Company the right to select its own officers independent of Parliament or King. In 1618 Virginia was granted yet another charter which gave Virginians the right to choose their own representatives who would make their laws. It was known as the General Assembly of Virginia and was composed of two houses — the Council chosen by the Virginia Company and the House of Burgesses chosen by the people. It was the beginning of representative government in the New World.

The Jamestown church had been rebuilt in 1617 and it was here that the first General Assembly met on July 30, 1619. This wooden church was the cradle of self-government in the new world. (The first brick church was built in 1639, probably on the same site as the 1617 church. Its foundations can be seen inside the present-day Memorial Church, built in 1907. The Old Church Tower connected to the Memorial Church was built in 1647.) The Burgesses sat in the choir of the church and the Council sat in the front pews.

A Virginia public school textbook of the 1960s states: "The men who came together in this first meeting of the first representative government in America wanted God to guide them in their work."[62] Proof of this is found in the official *Proceedings of the Virginia General Assembly*:

> The most convenient place we could finde to sitt in was the Quire [Choir] of the Churche Where Sir George Yeardley, the Governor, being sett downe in his accustomed place, those of the Counsel of Estate sate next him. . . . But forasmuche as men's affaires doe little prosper where God's service is

neglected, all the Burgesses tooke their places in the Quire till a prayer was said by Mr. Bucke, the Minister, that it would please God to guide and sanctifie all our proceedings to his owne glory and the good of this Plantation.[63]

The Assembly observed the Christian Sabbath by not conducting business on Sunday.[64]

One of the representatives at this meeting was also a clergyman, the Rev. William Wickham. This representative government was brought into being due in part to the efforts of Edwin Sandys, a vocal Puritan leader in the House of Commons who became the treasurer of the Virginia Company in 1619. During five days of meetings, the Virginia General Assembly abolished Dale's laws, gave toleration to dissenters, and created elected vestries. But they also decided that the Anglican Church in Virginia would tolerate no variations in their form of worship. The Puritan Rev. Mease decided to move away in order to have freedom to conduct services differently.

Other laws passed by the Assembly required everyone who owned weapons to bring them to church to protect against any Indian raids, prohibited the settlers from harming or injuring Indians, and required the towns and plantations to educate a certain number of Indian children "in true religion and civil course of life."[65] This latter provision turned out to be crucial to the survival of Jamestown in 1622.

Thanksgiving, and Henricus School and College

In addition to the meeting of the first General Assembly, other important events occurred in 1619. The first Thanksgiving celebrated in the New World took place on December 4 of that year at the Berkeley Plantation up the river from Jamestown. While not as well known as the Thanksgiving celebrated by the Pilgrims at Plymouth, it did take place a few years earlier. Captain John Woodlief and 37 other settlers held a short religious service on the day they arrived at Berkeley Plantation (in present-day Charles City) after a two-and-a-half-month voyage. The group of young men knelt down and gave thanks for their safe arrival in accordance with their charter, which stated, "Wee ordaine that the Day of our ship arrivall at the place assigned for Thanksgiving to Almighty God."[66] In 1963, President Kennedy officially recognized Berkeley Plantation as the site of the first Thanksgiving.

Late in 1619, the plan was made to send almost a hundred young women to Jamestown to provide wives for the colonists because, at the time, there were only a few women and many lonely men in Virginia. More families would add further stability and permanence to the society.

In 1618 the Virginia Company obtained a charter and a large tract of land from King James I for a college and school in Virginia. Its purpose was "education for the training of the Indians in the true knowledge of God and in some useful employment and to educate the children of the settlers who are now deprived of formal education."[67] By 1622 money had been raised, a teaching staff chosen, and construction begun on campus buildings. The Virginia Company published a book by Rev. John Brinsley on educational methods and a course of study appropriate for the school. In the *Dedicatorie* of the book Brinsley writes:

> To this purpose God having ordained schooles of learning to be a principall meanes to reduce a barbarous people to civilitie, and thereby to prepare them the better to receive the glorious Gospel of Jesus Christ; as also for the breeding and nourishing of such a holie Ministerie, with a wise and godlie Magistracie, and people to be perpetuallie preserved.[68]

The Massacre of 1622: Chanco Saves Jamestown

By 1618 both Pocahontas and her father, Chief Powhatan, had died. Without them the peace treaty was at risk, especially considering that the new chief, Opechancanough, blamed the English for the death by war, disease, and starvation of a large percentage of his people. (Over a 20 year period about 85% of his people died.) In 1621 the new governor of Virginia, Sir Francis Wyatt, heard that Opechancanough was planning to break the peace, and so he sent a messenger to renew the treaty. The chief acted as if he planned to fully keep the peace, but was really secretly plotting to kill all the colonists, who by this time were living on farms and in towns up and down the James River. John Smith recorded the tragic events, including God's providential protection of hundreds of the colonists. A Virginia school textbook of the early 1960s relates the event this way:

> Opechancanough's plot was so well planned and his secret so well kept that the English continued to trust the Indians completely. Two days before the massacre, the colonists were allowing the Indians to guide them through the forests. They were lending boats to the Indians. They did not know that the boats would be used by the Indians to cross the James River in order to make bloody plans with their friends. On Friday morning, March 22, 1622, the very day of the massacre, the Indians came as usual to the houses of the settlers with game and food to sell. Some of the Indians even sat down and ate breakfast with those they expected to murder.
>
> By eight o'clock in the morning, on that fearful Friday, the Indians had posted themselves in or near the homes of the English settlers. Then they fell upon the colonists all at the same time. The attack was so unexpected that many persons were unable to defend themselves. The Indians killed men, women, and children alike, sparing no one. They brutally killed their English friends and enemies alike. . . . Pocahontas' husband John Rolfe was one of the victims.[69]

Of the approximately 1240 persons living in Virginia at this time at least 347 were killed on this day of March 22, 1622.[70] This "Great Massacre" would have been even worse if God had not intervened through an Indian boy named Chanco (who is honored by a plaque inside the old church at Jamestown).

> Chanco had become a Christian, and he was grateful for the kindness the settlers had shown him. When his brother told him of the plans for the massacre, he passed on the dreadful news to his godfather and employer, Richard Pace. Pace, who lived across the river from Jamestown, slipped away in the night and warned Governor Wyatt. Because of this warning, the capital of Virginia and the plantations nearby had time to prepare for defense. The attacking Indians were unable to enter Jamestown or to surprise the people and the settlements near it.[71]

One early historian wrote: "The slaughter had beene universall, if God had not put it into the heart of an Indian, . . . lying in the house of one Pace, . . . [to] reveale it."[72] Understandably, this incident caused a great strain in the relationship of the settlers with the surrounding Indian tribes. Great caution was taken in any interaction with them. After the massacre, attempts to educate and spread the Christian faith among the Indians were greatly diminished. Henrico College, which was under construction, was destroyed by the Indians on March 22. The planting of a Christian college in Virginia would not be realized until 70 years later when William and Mary was established.

Slavery and Religious Persecution in Virginia

A few weeks after the meeting of the first representative assembly in 1619, a load of 20 Africans from a Dutch pirate ship landed at Jamestown. They were not enslaved, but became indentured servants, just like many of the white settlers. This provided them the means to acquire property on their own. They were granted 50 acres of land when freed from their indentures, enabling them to raise their own tobacco and crops. While the institution of slavery was common all the world over, the early settlers had no intention of propagating slavery in Virginia. As late as 1650 there were only about 300 Africans living in Virginia, about 1% of an estimated 30,000 population, and none were treated as slaves until 1654.

To purchase someone's labor as an indentured servant for a limited period of time was morally acceptable, and that is how many of the early English settlers came to the New World. Perpetual, race-based slavery was a cruel system and became a disgrace to the Christians who birthed the nation. If Virginia was a Christian colony in the beginning, how could this develop?

The old church tower at Jamestown dates from 1647 and in some ways this date marks the end of the more pure and vibrant period of Virginia's early faith. A key event that occurred around this time that led to the rise of slavery and also religious persecution in Virginia was the civil war in England. When Oliver Cromwell won the war against the King Charles I in 1649, thousands of refugees and supporters of the King fled to Virginia, causing the population to almost triple within ten years. These "Cavaliers" changed Virginia in two major ways.

First, being "gentlemen" who were not used to working for themselves, they were more inclined to accept slavery as a means of labor. Slavery was established in Virginia in 1654 when Anthony Johnson of Northampton County convinced the court that he was entitled to the lifetime services of John Casor, a black man. This was the first judicial approval of life servitude, except as punishment for a crime. Interestingly, Anthony Johnson was himself a black man, one of the original 20 brought to Jamestown in 1619.

With the approval of slavery in Virginia, the number of blacks increased from 300 to 2000 by the year 1670. There were 6000 by 1701 when the General Assembly tried to stop slave ships from coming to Virginia by placing a heavy tax on them. The English Parliament, however, overruled Virginia's law and the slave trade continued. By 1730 there were 28,500 blacks in Virginia, one fourth of the population.

The second change caused by the English Civil War was in the church in Virginia. The "Cavaliers" were enemies of the Puritans and were generally less devout in their faith. They insisted on Virginians conforming to a formal Anglican faith and increased persecution of dissenters. By law the Anglican Church was the official established denomination in Virginia, supported by the system of tithes collected like taxes from every citizen. Although this was the case, the Anglican church that developed in Virginia for the next century was still less hierarchical than the church in England and never had an English bishop. Church authority rested with the local church vestries that acted like boards of elders. Vestrymen were usually elected by the church members.

From the moment that King James took the charter away from Virginia in 1624 and made it a royal colony, the King appointed its governor. This practice lasted up to the American Revolution. However, the people still elected representatives to the House of Burgesses, even though the appointed royal governor had veto power over any legislation they enacted and could dissolve them at any time. Although the governor held a great amount of power, he needed the consent of the House of Burgesses for the governing of the colony. Without them he could not enact laws or collect taxes to which the people would agree. Thus, advancements in religious and civil liberty were occurring, even in the royal colony of Virginia.

The foundations of freedom were laid at Jamestown and came to fruition at the time of the American Revolution. The American Dream of a society with liberty, prosperity, and virtue eventually came to pass. The seeds of that dream were first planted at

Jamestown in 1607, but every one of the original thirteen colonies had similar Christian ideas in their foundations.

Chapter 5

Growth of the American Christian Republic

Christian seeds were planted in Virginia beginning in 1607. Similar seeds, some much purer, would be planted in all thirteen colonies in the generations that followed. These grew and produced the fruit of the American Dream.

The evidence that Christian ideas were at the core of the founding of the original American colonies is abundant. That evidence includes: the motive and Christian influence in colonization; the Christian foundation and source of our law; the nature and content of specific laws; the Christian nature of societal institutions of family, education, economics, private organizations; Christian thought and life of the Founders; the Christian power and form of our government; testimony of public actions and words; the central role of the Bible; and the fruit of obedience to the precepts of Christianity produced liberty, prosperity, and service.[1] (This evidence is examined in some of the other writings of the authors and in many other books, old and new.[2]) Christians colonized the states, wrote the laws and constitutions, started the schools and colleges, and served in leadership in every area of life.

One point of evidence for the Christian foundation of America is seen in the Christian nature of the founding civil documents of the original colonies. The source of civil law in a nation is of utmost importance because the source of law of a society is the God of that society. The source of law in America was the Bible and the Christian ideas issuing from it.

There were at least 128 different covenants, compacts, charters, and constitutions written during the colonization period of America — at least 86 constitution-like documents were written in the colonies before 1722 and at least 42 constitution-like documents written in England for the colonists before 1735.[3] These were the foundational civil documents of the original thirteen colonies, and hence of the states which comprised the United States of America. The Christian element is central and evident in almost all of these.

The Christian Nature of Colonial Civil Documents

Following are excerpts of a sampling of documents from each of the original thirteen colonies that reveal their Christian nature. Some of these are short covenants and agreements, some are oaths of rulers and citizens, and others are much longer documents that contain many civil ordinances. These are not generic religious statements, but specifically Christian and Bible centered.

Virginia

The Christian nature of the *First Charter of Virginia*, the *Articles, Laws, and Orders, Divine, Politic, and Martial for the Colony in Virginia, 1610-11*, and other civil writings were presented in the previous chapter. The Constitution for the Council and Assembly in Virginia, July 24, 1621, stated their primary endeavor was "in advancement and of the honor and service of Almighty God and the enlargement of His kingdom."[4]

Massachusetts

1. The Mayflower Compact, November 11, 1620

"In the name of God, Amen. We whose Names are under-written . . . Having undertaken for the glory of God, and advancement of the Christian Faith, and the Honor of our K[i]ng and Countrey, a Voyage to plant the first Colony in the Northern parts of Virginia; Do by these Presents, solemnly and mutually, in the presence of God, and one of another, Covenant and Combine our selves into a Civil Body Politick, for our better ordering and preservation, and furtherance of the ends aforesaid."[5]

2. The Salem Covenant of 1629

"We Covenant with the Lord and one with an other; and doe bynd our selves in the presence of God, to walke together in all his waies, according as he is pleased to reveale himselfe unto us in his Blessed word of truth."[6]

3. Agreement of the Massachusetts Bay Company at Cambridge, England, August 26, 1629

". . . every of us doth hereby freely and sincerely promise and bynd himselfe in the word of a Christian and in the presence of God who is the searcher of all hearts, that we will so really endevour the prosecucion of his worke, as by Gods assistaunce."[7]

4. The Watertown Covenant, July 30, 1630

"We . . . have undertaken for the promoting of his Glory and the Churches Good, and the Honour of our Blessed Jesus; . . . . and forsaking all Evil Ways, do give ourselves wholly unto the Lord Jesus, to do him faithful Service, observing and keeping all his Statutes, Commands, and Ordinances, in all Matters concerning our Reformation."[8]

5. The Oath of a Freeman, May 14, 1634

"I . . . doe heere sweare, by the great & dreadfull name of the evrlyving God. . . . Soe helpe mee God in the Lord Jesus Christ."[9]

6. The Massachusetts Body of Liberties, December 1641

Written by a Puritan minister, Nathaniel Ward, this document was the precusor of the U.S. Bill of Rights and was based upon

Mosaic law and English common law (which itself was Biblical in its origin). If incidences arose where there was no written civil ordinance, the document states the standard: "in case of the defect of a law in any partecular case by the word of god."[10]

7. The Laws and Liberties of Massachusetts, 1647

"In New-England . . . our Churches, and civil State have been planted, and growne up (like two twinnes) together like that of Israel in the wilderness by which wee were put in minde . . . not only to gather our Churches, and set up the Ordinances of Christ Jesus in them according to the Apostolick patterne by such light as the Lord graciously afforded us: but also withall to frame our civil Politie, and lawes according to the rules of his most holy word whereby each do help and strengthen other."[11]

"Considering that one end in planting these parts was to propagate the true Religion unto the Indians."[12]

The section on schools and making provisions for teachers in local towns begins: "It being one chief project of that old deluder, Satan, to keep men from the knowledge of the Scriptures."[13]

Rhode Island

1. Government of Pocasset, March 7, 1638

"We whose names are underwritten do here solemnly in the presence of Jehovah incorporate ourselves into a Bodie Politick and as he shall help, will submit our persons, lives and estates unto our Lord Jesus Christ, the King of Kings and Lord of Lords and to all those perfect and most absolute laws of his given us in his holy word of truth, to be guided and judged thereby. Exod. 24:3-4; 2 Cron. 11:3; 2 Kings 11:17."[14]

2. Organization of the Government of Rhode Island,
   March 16-19, 1642

"To the Execution of this office, I Judge myself bound before God to walk faithfully and this I profess in ye presence of God."[15]

When Roger Williams and others drew up the Providence Agreement (August 20, 1637) they did not use covenant language, as those at Pocasset and other localities did, but this was not for secular reasons, but due to their Christian conviction that using such terminology in a civil document was taking God's name in vain. Thus their Christian faith still governed their public as well as private actions (using the name Providence for the town founded by Williams shows this). In other words, lack of explicit acknowledgment of God in their civil documents did not reflect secularism or non-Christian belief.[16]

Following the reasoning of Williams and others concerning covenant language, the Acts and Orders of 1647 avoids appealing to God. For specific criminal offences it largely cites English law (which itself is derived mainly from Biblical ideas), but it does reference the Bible (Romans 1:27) as a standard when forbidding sodomy.[17]

Connecticut

1. Fundamental Orders of Connecticut, January 14, 1639

"Well knowning where a people are gathered togather the word of God requires that to mayntayne the peace and union of such a people there should be an orderly and decent Goverment established according to God . . . ; doe . . . enter into Combination and Confederation togather, to mayntayne and prsearve the liberty and purity of the gospell of our Lord Jesus wch we now prfesse."[18]

"The Oath of the Govrnor . . . . I . . . will further the execution of Justice according to the rule of Gods word; so helpe me God, in the name of the Lo: Jesus Christ."[19]

2. Connecticut Oath of Fidelity, 1640

"I A.B. being by the Prvidence of God an inhabitant wthin the Jurisdction of Conectecotte, doe acknowledge my selfe to be subject to the govrment thereof, and doe sweare by the great and dreadfull name of the evrliveing God to be true and faythfull unto the same; . . . So help me God in the Lo: Jesus Christ."[20]

3. Capitall Lawes of Connecticut, Established by the Generall Court the First of December, 1642

Many Scriptures from the Mosaic Law are given as the support for these capital laws.[21] This list of crimes for which people could possibly be put to death may seem harsh to people today, but were a major advancement compared to England and Europe, who had many more capital crimes. In America, everyone knew what the offences were, and if anyone was charged he had to be convicted in court. The death penalty was actually rare in America.

4. Preface to the General Laws and Liberties of Connecticut Colony Revised and Published by Order of the General Court Held at Hartford in October 1672

"We have endeavoured not onely to Ground our Capital Laws upon the Word of God, but also all our other Laws upon the Justice and Equity held forth in that word, which is a most perfect Rule."[22]

New Hampshire

1. Agreement of the Settlers at Exeter, July 5, 1639

"Wee . . . considering wth ourselves the holy will of god and our owne necessity, that we should not live whout wholsome lawes & government amongst us, . . . doe in the name of Christ & in the sight of God combine ourselves together, to erct & set up amongst us such government as shall be to our best discerning, agreeable to the will of god."[23]

The Rulers Oath: "You shall swear by the great and dreadful Name of the High God, Maker and Governor of Heaven and earth and by the Lord Jesus Christ, the Prince of the Kings and rulers of the earth, that in his Name and fear you will rule and govern his people according to the righteous will of God." The people took a similar oath.[24]

2. General Laws and Liberties of New Hampshire, March 16, 1680

Many of the "Cappitall Laws" quoted the Scriptures as justification for the death penalty in these incidences. If anyone profaned the "Lord's Day" he was fined or whipped. "If any . . . shall speak contempteously of the Holy Scriptures, or . . . behave himself contempteously of toward the Word of God preached, . . . or contempteously reproach ye wayes, churches or ordinances of Christ," he was fined or whipped.[25]

Maryland

1. The Charter of Maryland, June 20, 1632

The preamble to this charter issued by King Charles to Lord Calvert states how Calvert, "being animated with a laudable, and pious Zeal for extending the Christian Religion," was to start a new colony in America "partly occupied by Savages, having no knowledge of the Divine Being."[26]

2. Maryland Toleration Act, April 21, 1649

"fforasmuch as in a well governed and Xpian [Christian] Common Wea[l]th matters concerning Religion and the honor of God ought in the first place to bee taken, into serious consideracion and endeavoured to bee settled." The act of this Christian colony went on to establish one of the broadest definitions of religious freedom in the seventeenth century, protecting both Catholics and Protestants.[27]

New York

1. A Letter from Governor Richard Nicolls to the Inhabitants of Long Island, February 1665

In his letter establishing a legislature for New York, Governor Nicolls recommended the people choose rulers with Godly characteristics, the result of which would be "the propagation of true Religion amongst us."[28]

2. Charter of Liberties and Privileges, October 30, 1683

"Noe person or persons which professe ffaith in God by Jesus Christ Shall at any time be any wayes molested punished disquieted or called in Question for Difference in opinion."[29]

In New York Christian ministers were supported by public monies, which was true in many other colonies as well.

New Jersey

1. Fundamentals of West New Jersey, 1681

"Forasmuch as it hath pleased God, to bring us into this Province . . . that we may be a people to the praise and honour of his name, who hath so dealt with us, and for the good and welfare of our posterity to come."[30]

Pennylvania

1. Charter of Liberties and Frame of Government of the Province of Pennsylvania in America, May 5, 1682

"When the great and wise God had made the world, of all his creatures, it pleased him to chuse man his Deputy to rule it; and to fit him for so great a charge and trust, he did not only qualify him with skill and power, but with integrity to use them justly."[31]

William Penn, the author of this document, then presents the Biblical purpose of law and theory of government, quoting from the book of Romans and other Scriptures. He states "that government seems to me a part of religion itself, a thing sacred in its institution and end. For, if it does not directly remove the cause, it crushes the effects of evil, and is as such, (though a lower, yet) an emanation of the same Divine Power, that is both author and object of pure religion."[32]

This charter, as was similar in the other colonies, officially recognized "the Lord's Day," the Sabbath, where business was deferred till the next day.[33] The various laws presented in the charter were Biblical in their origin. Everyone who served in government, elected and appointed, "and all that have right to elect such Members, shall be such as possess faith in Jesus Christ."[34] Thus, only Christians could hold office and vote. This was true in other colonies as well.

2. Pennsylvania Charter of Liberties, 1701

"And that all persons who also profess to believe in Jesus Christ, the saviour of the world, shall be capable, notwithstanding their other persuasions and practices in point of conscience and religion, to serve this government in any capacity."[35]

North Carolina

1. The Fundamental Constitutions, 1669

"No man shall be permitted to be a freeman of Carolina or to have any estate or habitation within it that doth not acknowledge a God; and that God is publicly and solemnly to be worhipped." While the Church of England was recognized as the official church, religious freedom was acknowledged for others: "that Jews, heathens, and other dissenters from the purity of Christian religion may not be scared and kept at a distance from it; . . . and all those convincing methods of gentleness and meekness suitable to the rules and design of the Gospel, be won ever to embrace and unfeignedly receive the truth."[36]

South Carolina

The Fundamental Constitutions (see above) written by John Locke and Anthony Cooper governed the province of Carolina, which later divided into North and South Carolina.

1. Act to Ascertain the Manner and Form of Electing Members to Represent the Province, 1721

One qualification for voting or holding public office was "professing the Christian religion."[37] Officials "shall take the following oath on the holy evangelists. I, AB, so sincerely swear that I am duly qualified to be chosen and serve . . . . So help me God."[38]

Georgia

1. Act to Ascertain the Manner and Form of Electing Members to Represent the Inhabitants of This Province in the Commons House of Assembly, June 9, 1761

"Professing the christian religion and no other" was one qualification for holding elected office.[39]

The New England Confederation

The first attempt for several colonies to join together in union occurred in 1643 when Massachusetts, Plymouth, Connecticut, and New Haven approved a confederation. The Christian nature of this document is evident, stating: "Whereas we all came into these parts of America with one and the same end and aim, namely, to advance the kingdom of our Lord Jesus Christ and to enjoy the liberties of the Gospel in purity with peace." They entered into a "league of friendship . . . both for preserving and propogating the truth and liberties of the Gospel and for their own mutual safety and welfare."[40]

In addition to the specific Christian wording in these founding documents, they also contain ideas derived from a Biblical view of man and government, including such concepts as election of representatives, constitutionalism, separation of powers, religious liberty, property rights, no taxation without representation, and unalienable rights of man.

Again, the Christian nature of early laws and charters is just one of many evidences supporting the Christian founding of America. When considered altogether, the conclusion is apparent: without Christianity there would not be an American Republic. Christianity produced the seed — both men and ideas — that gave birth to the nation and the American Dream.

Chapter 6

Restoring and Preserving the American Dream

The Christian idea of God, man, family, truth, history, government, and education was the seed that produced the fruit of liberty, prosperity, justice, and virtue in America. It is what made America a success. We must sow this seed to get good fruit. Humanistic seeds will produce different fruit.

The restoration and preservation of the American Dream is dependent upon our understanding and acting upon this knowledge. The seed we plant determines the fruit we produce. We have been the most free and prosperous nation in history due to our Christian foundations. We cannot endure without this foundation.

America was built upon the Biblical understanding of liberty. Liberty is not freedom to do whatever we feel like doing, but it is freedom to do what God says we should be doing. God allows men to choose their own paths, but the end of their departing from God's way is death and destruction. Nations that reject God's truth and God's view of liberty will not prosper or advance. The most free nations are those in which individuals and institutions are most free to do that which God has said they are to do — that is, to perform their jurisdictional functions. The degree of liberty in a nation is measured by the freedom individuals, families, churches, and governmental bodies have to fulfill their

God-given purpose and responsibilities. Usurpation of authority by any institution leads to loss of liberty.

All societies must have shared values to function. The more Biblical those shared values are, the more freedom and prosperity the society will have, and the longer that nation will exist. The shared values of early America were the seven Christian ideas presented in Chapter 2. As the nation has gradually put these aside, we no longer have the shared values necessary to keep the union strong, free, and functioning properly. We have been embracing a different set of values, not rooted in a Christian worldview but a secular worldview. This has affected the nation in many ways.

One, we have been moving toward state control of education, health, and welfare, which has undermined the family and diminished Godly liberty. Two, we have moved toward more government control of property and business, with the same effects. Government has also been doing a poorer job in protecting citizens by not swiftly executing justice and, consequently, allowing the criminal element to flourish in society. There has also been a breakdown in the government controlling itself, seen, for example, in the judiciary usurping legislative authority. The government has also allowed immorality to increase (on television, in movies, in print, in art, in pornography stores), but has restricted Godly influence (diminishing faith in public life, restricting Christian expression).

In short, in recent years, the government has failed to do well what it is supposed to do — protect the righteous and punish evil doers — and attempted to do that which it is not supposed to do — that is, govern and control property, education, health, and welfare.

Nightmare or Dream?

The American Dream was rooted in the Founders' view that God gave certain truths to mankind that were self-evident. If we reject these fundamental truths that our nation was built upon and replace them with relativistic human standards, then that dream will become a nightmare. America has witnessed the rising nightmare in recent times. Most people in most nations throughout most of history have lived in the nightmare produced by man sitting in the place of God in his personal and civil life. As T. Robert Ingram stated, "The alternative to God's law must be the Apocalyptic horror of untrammeled human will insanely sitting in the temple of God where God ought to be."[1]

God's truth originally gave birth to the American Dream. Rejecting that truth has caused aspects of that dream to become a nightmare. The good news is that the dream can be restored. It begins in the heart and mind of each individual, as we remember what God has done, rely upon His grace to live and think rightly, and fulfill our duties and responsibilities in every sphere of life. Teaching others is how we plant the seeds of liberty.

It is primarily the role of the family and church to teach the Christian ideas upon which the nation was founded. The government must not suppress, but encourage the church and family in this mission. Education is the central institution to pass on the values to future generations and, thus, education ought to be governed by families and the private sector. The Caesar mentality in America has led to the government assuming the primary role in educating citizens. Part of the fruit of teaching Biblical truth will be a diminishing role of government in education. Yet, as long as there are government schools, they should encourage the teaching of the seven ideas that made America successful. Without these ideas being passed on, the American Dream cannot be sustained. America will become something else, with less liberty, virtue, prosperity, and justice.

The fullness of the American Dream can once again become a reality. But we must remember, repent, prepare our children and all citizens, and return the nation to its original covenant. This will be for the good of our nation, ourselves, our posterity, and for God's plan to spread liberty throughout the world.

Appendix 1

Excerpts from:

Articles, Laws, and Orders, Divine, Politic, and Martial for the Colony in Virginia, 1610-11

By Sir Thomas Gates, Sir Thomas West and Sir Thomas Dale

. . . for the glory of God. . . .

1. First since we owe our highest and supreme duty, our greatest, and all our allegiance to him, from whom all power and authority is derived, and flows as from the first, and only fountain, and being especial soldiers impressed in this sacred cause, we must alone expect our success from him, who is only the blesser of all good attempts, the King of kings, the commander of commanders, and Lord of Hosts, I do strictly command and charge all Captains and Officers, of what quality or nature soever, whether commanders in the field, or in the town, or towns, forts or fortresses, to have a care that the Almighty God be duly and daily served, and that thy call upon their people to hear Sermons, as that also they diligently frequent Morning and Evening prayer themselves by their own exemplar and daily life, and duty herein, encouraging others thereunto, and that such, who shall often and wilfully absent themselves, be duly punished according to the martial law in that case provided.

2. That no man speak impiously or maliciously, against the holy and blessed Trinity, or any of the three persons, that is to say, against God the Father, God the Son, and God the holy Ghost, or

against the known Articles of the Christian faith, upon pain of death.

3. That no man blaspheme God's holy name upon pain of death, or use unlawful oaths, taking the name of God in vain, curse, or ban, upon pain of severe punishment for the first offence so committed, and for the second, to have a bodkin thrust through his tongue, and if he continue the blaspheming of Gods holy name, for the third time so offending, he shall be brought to a martial court, and there receive censure of death for his offence...

5. No man shall speak any word, or do any act, which may tend to the derision, or despite of Gods holy word upon pain of death: Nor shall any man unworthily demean himself unto any Preacher, or Minister of the same, but generally hold them in all reverent regard, and dutiful entreaty, otherwise he the offender shall openly be whipped three times, and ask public forgiveness in the assembly of the congregation three several Sabbath days.

6. Every man and woman duly twice a day upon the first tolling of the Bell shall upon the working days repair unto the Church, to hear divine Service upon pain of losing his or her days allowance for the first omission, for the second to be whipped, and for the third to be condemned to the Galleys for six Months. Likewise no man or woman shall dare to violate or break the Sabbath by any gaming, public, or private abroad, or at home, but duly sanctify and observe the same, both himself and his family, by preparing themselves at home with private prayer, that they may be the better fitted for the public, according to the commandments of God, and the orders of our Church, as also every man and woman shall repair in the morning to the divine service, and Sermons preached upon the Sabbath day, and in the afternoon to divine service, and Catechising, upon pain for the first fault to lose their provision, and allowance for the whole week following, for the second to lose the said allowance, and also to be whipped, and for the third to suffer death.

7. All Preachers or Ministers within this our Colony, or Colonies, shall in the Forts, where they are resident, after divine Service, duly preach every Sabbath day in the forenoon, and Catechise in the afternoon, and weekly say the divine service, twice every day, and preach every Wednesday. . . .

10. No man shall be found guilty of Sacrilege, which is a Trespass as well committed in violating and abusing any sacred ministry, duty or office of the Church, irreverently, or prophanely, as by being a Church robber, to filch, steal or carry away any thing out of the Church appertaining thereunto, or unto any holy, and consecrated place, to the divine Service of God, which no man should do upon pain of death. . . .

12. No manner of person whatsoever, shall dare to detract, slander, calumniate, or utter unseemly, and unfitting speeches, . . . against the zealous endeavours, & intentions of the whole body of Adventurers for this pious and Christian Plantation. . . .

13. . . . the word of God (which ties every particular and private man, for conscience sake to obedience, and duty of the Magistrate, and such as shall be placed in authority over them). . .

33. There is not one man nor woman in this Colony now present, or hereafter to arrive, but shall give up an account of his and their faith, and religion, and repair unto the Minister, that by his conference with them, he may understand, and gather, whether heretofore they have been sufficiently instructed, and catechised in the principles and grounds of Religion, whose weakness and ignorance herein, the Minister finding, and advising them in all love and charity, to repair often unto him, to receive therein a greater measure of knowledge, if they shall refuse so to repair unto him, and he the Minister give notice thereof unto the Governor, or that chief officer of that town or fort, wherein he or she, the parties so offending shall remain, the Governor shall cause the offender for his first time of refusal to be whipped. . . .

Every Minister or Preacher shall every Sabbath day before Catechising, read all these laws and ordinances, publicly in the assembly of the congregation. . .

The Summary of the Martial Laws.

. . . the divine Majesty of God. . . .

He that shall take the name of God in vain . . . shall be committed to prison, there to lie in Irons for three days, for the second time so offending, he shall be whipped, and for the third time so offending he shall be condemned to the Galleys for one year. . . .

. . . all good and upright men that have the fear of God, and his service, and their own honor in regard, will demean themselves no less, then according to the dignity of their place, and charge of their command, the united powers of his Lordships knowledge, being so full of approved nobleness, and the well known, and long time exercised grounds of Piety. . . .

Instructions of the Martial for better enabling of the Colonel or Governor, to the executing of his or their charges in this present Colony the 22. of June. 1611.

. . . to honor God. . . .

. . . what well-doing can be greater then to be stocks & authors of a people that shall serve and glorify God, which is the end of all our Creation, & to redeem them from ignorance and infidelity, to the true knowledge and worship of God, whereby you are made partakers of this promise, that they which lead others into Righteousness, shall shine like the stars in the firmament. . . .

. . . impious and malicious speaking against the holy and blessed Trinity, Blasphemy, and taking Gods holy name in vain, traiterous words against his majesty's person, or Royal Authority, unreverent Demeanor towards the Ministers and preachers of the same.

Instructions of the Marshal for the better enabling of the Captain of the watch, to the executing of his charge in this present Colony. the 22. of June. 1611.

. . . Out of this example commended unto us by the holy writ, it may well be, that many Officers are still continued in all united societies, religious and well governed: having then thus religion, beside prescription and reason, (which mine own breeding has taught me how to make the best use of) to be my guides in this new settlement. . . .

If it shall so be that he be Capt. of the watch upon Sunday, it shall be his duty to see that the Sabbath be no ways prophaned, by any disorders, gaming, drunkeness, intemperate meeting, or such like, in public or private, in the streets or within the houses.

It shall be his duty half an hour before the divine service, morning & evening, to shut the Ports and place Sentinels, and the Bell having tolled the last time, he shall search all the houses of the town , to command every one, of what quality soever (the sick and hurt excepted) to repair to Church, after which he shall accompany all the guards with their arms, (himself being last) into the Church, and lay the keys before the Governor.

Instructions of the Marshal , for the better enabling of a Captain, to the executing of his charge in this present Colony. June the 22. 1611

. . . the great Judge of Judges, who leaves not unpunished the sins of the people. . . .

. . . all their actions and practises which shall break forth in them, contrary to the divine prescriptions of Piety and Religion: their perjuries, blasphemies, prophaneness, riots, and what disorders soever, and generally all their breaches of both the sacred Tables, divine, and moral, to GOD and man, and in this place most especially, where the work assumed, has no other ends but such as may punctually advance the glory, and propagation of the heavenly goodness, for which so many religious laws and ordinances are established, and declared; . . . and bring poor misbelieving miscreants, to the knowledge of the eternal kingdom of God. . . .

how careful he is to please God, who must bless all that he undertakes, and walk himself in a noble example of Justice and truth; . . .

. . . except a man be virtuous and religious indeed, and that virtue extend itself to example. . .

. . . all his company (unless his Sentinels) and assembled together, humbly present themselves on their knees, and by faithful and zealous prayer unto almighty God commend themselves and their endeavours to his merciful protection. . . .

. . . there, with public prayer, give unto almighty God humble thanks and praises, for his merciful and safe protection that night, and commend himself and his, to his no less merciful protection and safeguard for the day following. . . .

Instructions of the Marshal for the better enabling of a Corporal unto the discharge of his duty in this present Colony, June the 22. 1611.

. . . his care shall be to attend his squadron to the usual works and day–labors , and unto frequent prayers, and the divine service at all times. . . .

Instructions of the Marshal for the better enabling of a private soldier, to the executing of his duty in this present Colony. June 22. 1611

It is requisite that he who will enter into this function of a soldier, that he dedicate himself wholly for the planting and establishing of true religion. . . .

. . . he ought to be diligent, careful , vigilant and obedient, and principally to have the fear of God. . . .

He must be careful to serve God privately and publicly; for all profession are thereunto tied, that carry hope with them to prosper, and none more highly then the soldier, for he is ever in the mouth of death, and certainly he that is thus religiously armed, fights more confidently and with greater courage, and is thereby protected through manifold dangers, and otherwise unpreventable events.

He must be no blasphemer nor swearer, for such an one is contemptible to God and the world, and shall be assured to be found out and punished by the divine Justice: whereof we have instant examples.

. . . true religion ordained of God, which binds the soldier to observe justice, loyalty , faith, constancy , patience, silence, and above all, obedience. . . .

Appendix 2

A Prayer duly said Morning and Evening upon the Court of Guard, either by the Captain of the watch himself, or by some one of his principal officers.

Merciful Father, and Lord of heaven and earth, we come before thy presence to worship thee in calling upon thy name, and giving thanks unto thee, and though our duties and our very necessities call us here unto: Yet we confess our hearts to be so dull and untoward, that unless thou be merciful to us to teach us how to pray, we shall not please thee, nor profit our selves in these duties. We therefore most humbly beseech thee to raise up our hearts with thy good spirit, and so to dispose us to prayer, that with true fervency of heart, feeling of our wants, humbleness of mind, and faith in thy gracious promises, we may present our suits acceptably unto thee by our Lord and Saviour Jesus Christ.

And thou our Father of all mercies, that hast called us unto thee, hear us and pity thy poor servants, we have indeed sinned wonderously against thee through our blindness of mind, prophaneness of spirit, hardness of heart, self love, worldliness, carnal lusts, hypocrisy, pride, vanity, unthankfulness, infidelity, and other our native corruptions, which being bred in us, and with us, have defiled us even from the womb, and unto this day, and have broken out as plague sores into unnumberable transgressions of all thy holy laws, (the good ways whereof we have wilfully declined,) & have many times displeased thee, and our own consciences in choosing those things which thou hast most justly & severely forbidden us. And besides all this we have outstood the gracious time and means of our conversion, or at least not stooped and humbled our selves before thee, as we ought, although we have wanted none of those helps, which thou vouchsafest unto thy wandering children to fetch them home withall, for we have had together with thy glorious works, thy word calling upon us without, and thy spirit within, and have been solicited by promises, by threatenings, by blessings, by chastisings, & by examples, on all hands: And yet our corrupted spirits cannot become wise before thee, to humble themselves, and to take heed as we ought, and wish to do. Wherefore O Lord God, we do acknowledge thy patience to have been infinite and incomparable, in that thou hast been able to hold thy hands from revenging thy self upon us thus long, & yet pleasest to hold open the door of grace, that we might come in unto thee and be saved.

And now O blessed Lord God, we are desirous to come unto thee, how wretched soever in our selves, yea our very wretchedness sends us unto thee: unto thee with whom the fatherless, and he that has no helper finds mercy, we come to thee in thy Sons name not daring to come in our own: In his name that came for us, we come to thee, in his mediation whom thou hast sent: In him O Father, in whom thou hast professed thy self to be well pleased, we come unto thee, and do most humbly beseech thee to pity us, & to save us for thy mercies sake in him.

O Lord our God our sins have not outbidden that blood of thy holy Son which speaks for our pardon, nor can they be so infinite, as thou art in thy mercies, & our hearts (O God thou seest them,) our hearts are desirous to have peace with thee, and war with our lusts, and wish that they could melt before thee, and be dissolved into godly mourning for all that filth that has gone through them, and defiled them. And our desires are now to serve and please thee, and our purposes to endeavour it more faithfully, we pray thee therefore for the Lord Jesus sake seal up on our consciences thy gracious pardon of all our sins past, and give us to feel the consolation of this grace shed abroad in our hearts for our eternal comfort and salvation: and that we may know this persuasion to be of thy spirit, and not of carnal presumption, (blessed God) let those graces of thy spirit, which do accompany salvation, be powred out more plentifully upon us, increase in us all godly knowledge, faith, patience, temperance, meekness, wisdom, godliness, love to thy Saints and service, zeal of thy glory, judgement to discern the difference of good & ill, and things present which are temporary, and things to come which are eternal.

Make us yet at the last wise-hearted to lay up our treasure in heaven, and to set our affections more upon things that are above, where Christ sits at thy right hand: And let all the vain and transitory enticements of this poor life, appear unto us as they are, that our hearts may no more be entangled and bewitched with the love of them. O Lord, O God, our God, thou hast dearly bought us for thine own self, give us so honest hearts as may be glad to yield the possession of thine own. And be thou so gracious, as yet to take them up, though we have desperately held thee out of them in times past, and dwell in us, and reign in us by thy spirit, that we may be sure to reign with thee in thy glorious kingdom, according to thy promise through him that has purchased that inheritance for all that trust in him.

And seeing thou do so promise these graces to us, as that thou requirest our industry and diligence in the use of such means as serve thereto (good Lord) let us not so cross our prayers for grace, as not to seek that by diligence, which we make show to seek by prayer, least our own ways condemn us of hypocrisy. Stir us up therefore (O Lord) to the frequent use of prayer, to reading, hearing, and meditating of thy holy word, teach us to profit by the conversation of thy people, and to be profitable in our own, make us wise to apprehend all oportunites of doing or receiving spiritual good, strengethen us with grace to observe our hearts and ways, to contain them in good order, or to reduce them quickly, let us never think any company so good as thine, nor any time so well spent, as that which is in thy service, and beautifying of thine Image in our selves or others.

Particularly we pray thee open our eyes to see our natural infirmities, and to discover the advantages which Satan gets thereby. And give us care to strive most, where we are most assaulted and damaged. And thou O God, that hast promised to bless thine own ordinances, bless all things unto us, that we may grow in grace & in knowledge, and so may shine as light in this dark world, giving good example to all men, and may in our time lie down in peace of a good conscience, embalmed with a good report, and may leave thy blessings entailed unto ours after us for an inheritance.

These O Father, are our special suits, wherein we beseech thee to set forth the wonderful riches of thy grace towards us, as for this life, and the things thereof, we crave them of thee so far as may be for our good, and thy glory, beseeching thee to provide for us as unto this day in mercy. And when thou wilt humble or exalt us, govern us so long, and so far in all conditions and changes, as we may cleave fast unto thee our God unchangeably, esteeming thee our portion & sufficient inheritance for evermore. Now what graces we crave for our selves, which are here before thy presence, we humbly beg for all those that belong unto us, and that by duty or promise we own our prayers unto, beseeching thee to be as gracious unto them, as unto our own souls, and specially to such of them, as in respect of any present affliction or temptation may be in special need of some more speedy help or comfort from thy mighty hand.

Yea our Lord God we humbly desire to bless with our prayers the whole Church more specially our nation, and therein the kings Majesty our Sovereign, his Queen and royal seed, with all that be in authority under him, beseeching thee to follow him and them with those blessings of thy protection and direction, which may preserve them safe from the malice of the world, and of Satan, and may yield them in their great places faithful to thee for the good of thy people, and their own eternal happiness and honor.

We beseech thee to furnish the Churches with faithful and fruitful ministers, and to bless their lives and labors for those merciful uses, to which thou hast ordained them, sanctify thy people O God, and let them not deceive themselves with a formality of religion in steed of the power thereof, give them grace to profit both by those favors, and by those chastisements which thou hast sent successively or mixedly amongst them. And Lord repress that rage of sin, and prophaneness in all Christian states which breeds so much Apostacy and defection, threatening the taking away of this light from them: Confound thou O God all the counsel and practices of Satan and his ministers, which are or shall be taken up against thee, and the kingdom of thy dear son. And call in the Jews together with the fullness of the gentiles, that thy name may be glorious in all the world, the days of iniquity may come to an end, and we with all thine elect people may come to see thy face in glory, and be filled with the light thereof for evermore.

And now O Lord of mercy, O Father of the spirits of all flesh, look in mercy upon the Gentiles, who yet know thee not, O gracious God be merciful to us, and bless us, and not us alone, but let thy ways be known upon earth, & thy saving health amongst all nations: we praise thee, and we bless thee: But let the people praise thee O God, yea let all the people praise thee, and let these ends of the world remember themselves and turn to thee the God of their salvation. And seeing thou hast honored us to choose us out to bear thy name unto the Gentiles: we therefore beseech thee to bless us, and this our plantation. which we and our nation have begun in thy fear, & and for thy glory. We know O Lord, we have the devil and all the gates of hell against us, but if thou O Lord be on our side, we care not who be against us. O therefore vouchsafe to be our God, & let us be a part and portion of thy people, confirm thy covenant of grace & mercy with us, which thou hast made to thy Church in Christ Jesus. And seeing Lord the highest end of our plantation here, is to set up the standard, & display the banner of Jesus Christ, even here where satans throne is Lord, let our labor be blessed in laboring the conversion of the heathen. And because thou usest not to work such mighty works by unholy means, Lord sanctify our spirits, & give us holy hearts, that so we may be thy instruments in this most glorious work: lord inspire our souls with thy grace, kindle in us zeal of thy glory: fill our hearts with thy fear, & our tongues with thy praise, furnish us all from the highest to the lowest with all gifts & graces needful not only for our salvation, but for the discharge of our duties in our several places, adorn us with the garments of Justice, mercy, love, pity, faithfulness, humility, & all virtues, & teach us to abhor all vice, that our lights may so shine before these heathen, that they may see our good works, & so be brought to glorify thee our heavenly Father. And seeing Lord we profess our selves thy servants, & are about thy work, Lord bless us, arm us against difficulties, strength us against all base thoughts & temptations, that may make us look back again. And seeing by thy motion & work in our hearts, we have left our warm nests at home, & put our lives into our hands principally to honor thy name, & advance the kingdom of thy son, Lord give us leave to commit our lives into thy hands: let thy Angels be about us, & let us be as Angels of God sent to this people, And so bless us Lord, & so prosper all our proceedings, that the heathen may never say unto us, where is now your God: Their Idols are not so good as silver & gold, but lead & copper, & the works of their own hands. But thou Jehovah art our God, & we are the works of thy hands: O then let Dagon fall before thy Ark, let Satan be confounded at thy presence, & let the heathen see it & be ashamed, that they may seek thy face, for their God is not our God, themselves being Judges. Arise therfore O Lord, & let thine enemies be scattered, & let them that hate thee fly before thee: As the smoke vanishes, so let Satan & his delusions come to nought & as wax melts before the fire, so let wickedness, superstition, ignorance & idolatry perish at the presence of thee our God. And whereas we have by undertaking this plantation undergone the reproofs of the base world, insomuch as many of our own brethren laugh us to scorn, O Lord we pray thee fortify us against this temptation: let Sanballat, & Tobias, Papists & players, & such other Amonists & Horonits the scum & dregs of the earth, let them mock such as help to build up the walls of Jerusalem, and they that be filthy, let them be filthy still, & let such swine still wallow in their mire, but let not the rod of the wicked fall upon the lot of the righteous, let not them put forth their hands to such vanity, but let them that fear thee, rejoice & be glad in thee, & let them know, that it is thou O Lord, that reigns in England, & unto the ends of the world. And seeing this work must needs expose us to many miseries, & dangers of soul & body, by land & sea, O Lord we earnestly beseech thee to receive us into thy favor & protection, defend us from the delusion of the devil, the malice of the heathen, the invasions of our enemies, & mutinies & dissentions of our own people, knit our hearts altogether in faith & fear of thee, & love one to another, give us patience, wisdom & constancy to go on through all difficulties & temptations, til this blessed work be accomplished, for the honor of thy name, & glory of the Gospel of Jesus Christ: That when the heathen do know thee to be their God, and Jesus Christ to be their salvation, they may say, blessed by the King & Prince of England, & blessed be the English nation, and blessed for ever be the most high God, possessor of heaven & earth, that sent them amongst us: And here O Lord we do upon the knees of our hearts offer thee the sacrifice of praise & thanksgiving, for that thou hast moved our hearts to undertake the performance of this blessed work, with the hazard of our person, and the hearts of so may hundreds of our nation to assist it with means & provision, and with their holy prayers, Lord look mercifully upon them all, and for that portion of their substance which they willingly offer for thy honor & service in this action, recompence it to them and theirs, and reward it seven fold into their bosoms with better blessings: Lord bless England our sweet native country, save it from Popery, this land from heathenism, & both from Atheism. And Lord hear their prayers for us, and us for them, and Christ Jesus our glorious Mediator for us all. Amen.

End Notes

Chapter 1

1. B.F. Morris, *The Christian Life and Character of the Civil Institutions of the United States*, Philadelphia: George W. Childs, 1864, p. 109.

2. Morris, pp. 41-42.

3. Mark A. Beliles and Stephen K. McDowell, *America's Providential History*, Charlottesville: Providence Foundation, 1989, p. 17.

4. Ibid., p. 17.

5. John Winthrop, *A Modell of Christian Charity*, 1630, Old South Leaflets, No. 207, Boston: The Old South Association.

6. William Penn, Letter to James Harrison, August 25, 1681, *Remember William Penn*, compiled by the William Penn Tercentenary committee, Harrisburg: Commonwealth of Pennsylvania, 1945, p. 77.

7. Timothy Lamer, "Better off French," *World Magazine*, May13, 2006, p. 33.

8. Ibid.

9. Ibid.

10. "France dismantles 35-hour work week," *The Daily Progress*, Charlottesville, Virginia, Tuesday, March 22, 2005, p. A9.

11. "Son's name worth jail, mom says," *The Commercial Appeal*, Memphis, Thursday, December 24, 1998.

12. "Socialist pigs," *World Magazine*, February 15, 2003, p. 12.

13. E.G.R. Taylor, editor, *The Original Writings and Correspondence of the Two Richard Hakluyts*, Vol. 2, London: Hakluyt Society, 1935, p. 318.

14. "The First Charter of Virginia," in *Sources of Our Liberties*, Richard L. Perry, editor, American Bar Foundation, 1952, pp. 39-40.

Chapter 2

1. Madison Papers, Series 2, Library of Congress, quoted in K. Alan Snyder, *Defining Noah Webster, Mind and Morals in the Early Republic*, New York: University Press of America, 1990, p. 253.

2. Election Sermon given at Charleston, MA on April 25, 1799.

3. Cited in B.F. Morris, *Christian Life and Character of the Civil Institutions of the United States*, p. 328.

4. See Stephen McDowell, *The Ten Commandments and Modern Society*, Charlottesville: Providence Foundation, 2000.

5. Gene Edward Veith, "The end of humanism," *World Magazine*, April 22, 2006, p. 30.

6. Noah Webster, *A Manual of Useful Studies*, New Haven: S. Babcock, 1839, p. 77-78.

7. Elias Boudinot, "Oration at Elizabethtown, New Jersey, on the Fourth of July, 1793." *American Eloquence: A Collection of Speeches and Addresses, by the Most Eminent Orators of America*, New York: D. Appleton and Company, 1858, Vol. 1, p. 266.

8. See Stephen McDowell, *Building Godly Nations*, Chapter 11, "The Changing Nature of Law in America," Charlottesville: Providence Foundation, 2004, pp. 183 ff.

9. Andrew W. Young, *First Lessons in Civil Government,* Auburn, N.Y.: H. And J.C. Ivison, 1846, p. 16.

10. Thomas Paine, "Declaration of Rights," *The Writings of Thomas Paine*, Collected and edited by Daniel Conway, New York: G.P. Putnam's Sons, Vol.3 , p. 129-130.

11. See McDowell, *Building Godly Nations*, Chapter 7, "The Influence of the Bible on the Development of American Constitutionalism."

12. See ibid., Chapter 1.

13. James Rose, *A Guide to American Christian Education,* Camarillo, CA: American Christian History Institute, 1987, p. 455.

14. From Charles Rollin's *Ancient History*, quoted in "The Education of John Quincy Adams," by Rosalie J. Slater, in *The Christian History of the American Revolution*, Verna M. Hall, compiler, San Francisco: Foundation for American Christian Education, 1976, p. 605.

15. George Bancroft, *Memorial Address on the Life and Character of Abraham Lincoln*, Delivered at the Request of Both Houses of the Congress of America, Before Them in the House of Representatives at Washington, on the 12th of February, 1866, Washington: Government Printing Office, 1866, pp. 3-4.

16. See McDowell, *Building Godly Nations*, p. 21.

17. Boudinot, p. 265.

18. Robert C. Winthrop, "Address to Massachusetts Bible Society Meeting, May 28, 1849", *Addresses and Speeches on Various Occasions*, Boston: Little, Brown & Co., 1852, p. 172.

19. Richard Morris, editor, *Significant Documents in United States History,* Vol. 1, New York: Van Nostrand Reinhold Co., 1969, p. 15-16.

20. *The Laws of the Pilgrims, 1672 & 1685,* A Facsimile Edition, Pulbished by Michael Glazier and the Pilgrim Society, 1977.

21. *Maxims of Washington*, compiled by John Frederick Schroeder, New York: D. Appleton & Co., 1854, p. 341.

22. Stephen McDowell wrote this chapter.

23. See Matthew 12:17-21; John 19:11; *Building Godly Nations*, pp. 43 ff.; *America's Providential History,* pp. 29 ff.

24. Rom. 13:1-5; 1 Pet. 2:13-14; for more on a Biblical view of government see *Building Godly Nations*, Chapter 3; Stephen McDowell and Mark Beliles, *Liberating the Nations*, chapters 1, 11, Charlottesville: Providence Foundation, 1995.

25. Noah Webster, *History of the United States*, New Haven: Durrie & Peck, 1833, p. v.

26. Benjamin Rush, *Essays, Literary, Moral and Philosophical*, Philadelphia: printed by Thomas and William Bradford, 1806, p. 93.

27. Rush, p. 113.

28. Richard Morris, editor, *Significant Documents in United States History,* p. 20.

29. From *New Englands First Fruits, 1643*, in *Teaching and Learning America's Christian History* by Rosalie Slater, San Francisco: Foundation for American Christian Education, 1980, p. vii.

30. *The Life and Public Services of Samuel Adams*, by William V. Wells, Boston: Little, Brown & Co., 1865, Vol. III, p. 301.

Chapter 3

1. Matthew Page Andrews, *The Soul of a Nation*, New York: Charles Scribner's Sons,1944, p. 1-2.

2. George Bruner Parks, *Richard Hakluyt and the English Voyages*, New York: American Geographical Society, 1928, p. xiv.

3. Andrews, p. 6.

4. Andrews, p. 2.

5. E.G.R. Taylor, editor, *The Original Writings and Correspondence of the Two Richard Hakluyts*, Vol. 2, London: Hakluyt Society, 1935, p. 211.

6. Ibid.; see *The Principal Navigations, Voyages, Traffiques & Discoveries of the English Nation*, by Richard Hakluyt, Vol 12, New York: The Macmillan Co., 1905, p. 32 for more on this.

7. Taylor, p. 318 and Old South Leaflets, No. 122, *England's Title to North America*, from Hakluyt's *Discourse Concerning Westerne Planting*, p. 12, Boston: Old South Meeting-house.

8. Andrews, p. 3.

9. Old South Leaflets, No. 122, p. 16.

10. This version with modern spelling is from *Hakluyt's Voyages to the New World*, edited by David Freeman Hawke, Bobbs-Merrill Co., pp 3-5. See also, Old South Leaflets, No. 122, and Samuel Eliot Morison, *The European Discovery of America, the Northern Voyages*, New York: Oxford Univ. Press, 1971, p. 556-557.

11. Old South Leaflets, No. 122, p. 14.

12. Hawke, p. 3-4.

13. Old South Leaflets, p. 15.

14. From a brief biography on Richard Hakluyt by Walter Raleigh in *The Principal Navigations*, Vol. 12, p. 74-75.

15. Ibid.

16. Ibid., p. 84.

17. Ibid., p. 85.

18. Old South Leaflets, p. 15.

19. Taylor, p. 176.

20. Taylor, p. 178.

21. Ibid.

22. Taylor, p. 211.

23. Taylor, p. 214-215.

24. Taylor, p. 215.

25. Taylor, p. 216.

26. Taylor, p. 318.

27. Parks, p. 88.

28. Morison, p. 560.

29. Hakluyt wrote to Raleigh in 1587 concerning his efforts to establish a settlement, which were underway at that time. He noted that

men have different motives for discovery and colonization. "Some seeke authoritie and places of commandement," others seek worldly gain, and

> that often times by dishonest and unlawfull meanes, the fewest number the glorie of God and the saving of the soules of the poore and blinded infidels. Yet because divers honest and well disposed persons are entred already into this your businesse, and that I know you meane hereafter to sende some such good Churchmen thither, as may truly say with the Apostle to the Savages (2 Cor. 12:14), Wee seeke not yours but you: I conceive great comfort of the successe of this your action, hoping that the Lorde, whose power is wont to bee perfected in weakenesse, will blesse the feeble foundations of your building. Onely bee you of a valiant courage and faint not, as the Lorde sayd unto Josue (Josue 1:6), exhorting him to proceede on forward in the conquest of the land of promise, and remember that private men have happily wielded and waded through as great enterprises as this, with lesser meanes then those which God in his mercie hath bountifully bestowed upon you.
>
> ("Hakluyt's Dedication to Ralegh, 1587," in *The First Colonists, Documents on the Planting of the First English Settlements in North America*, 1584-1590, edited by David B. Quinn and Alison M. Quinn, Raleigh: North Carolina Department of Cultural Resources, 1982, 1995, pp. 90-91.)

30. Richard Hakluyt, *A Selection of The Principal Voyages, Traffiques and Discoveries of the English Nation*, compiled by Laurence Irving, New York: Alfred A. Knopf, 1926, p. xi-xii.

31. Andrews, p. 4-5.

32. Richard Hakluyt, *A Selection ...*, compiled by Irving, p.260. The quotes that follow up to end note 34 are also from this work, pp. 285-292.

33. Ibid., p. 292.

34. "The First Charter of Virginia," in *Sources of Our Liberties*, Richard L. Perry, editor, New York: American Bar Foundation, 1952, pp. 39-40.

35. Parks, p. 256.

36. Andrews, p. 57.

37. *The Jamestown Voyages under the First Charter 1606-09*, Vol. 1, edited by Philip Barbour, Cambridge: University Press, 1969, p. 115.

38. Barbour, p. 118.

39. Alexander Brown, *The First Republic in America*, Boston: Houghton, Mifflin, and Co., 1898. p. 80-81.

40. Brown, p. 50.

41. Brown, p. 52.

42. Brown, p. 64.

43. Andrews, p. 54.

44. Andrews, p. 56.

45. See Andrews, pp. 77-79, 68-71.

46. Morison, p. 561.

47. The Will of Richard Hakluyt, 1612, in Taylor, Vol. 2, p. 506.

Chapter 4

1. E.G.R. Taylor, editor, *The Original Writings and Correspondence of the Two Richard Hakluyts*, Vol. 2, London: Hakluyt Society, 1935, p. 318 and Old South Leaflets, No. 122, *England's Title to North America*, from Hakluyt's *Discourse Concerning Westerne Planting*, p. 12, Boston: Old South Meeting-house.

2. "The First Charter of Virginia," in *Sources of Our Liberties*, pp. 39-40.

3. Andrews, p. 54.

4. Engraved on the Monument. Also in, John Fiske, *Old Virginia and Her Neighbors*, Vol. 1, New York, Houghton, Mifflin, and Co., 1897, p. 76. See also Bishop Meade, *Old Churches, Ministers and Families of Virginia*, Vol. 1, Philadephia: J.B. Lippincott Company, 1857, p. 64. See also Andrews, p. 56.

5. Benjamin Hart, *Faith and Freedom, The Christian Roots of American Liberty*, Lewis and Stanley, Dallas, 1988, p. 139.

6. John Smith, *A True Relation, 1608*, in *Narratives of Early Virginia, 1606-1625*, Lyon Gardiner Tyler, Editor, New York: Barnes & Noble, Inc., 1950, p. 32.

7. George Bruner Parks, *Richard Hakluyt and the English Voyages*, New York: American Geographical Society, 1928, p. 256; and Andrews, p. 57.

8. Ralph Hamor, *A True Discourse of the Present State of Virginia*, reprinted from the London edition, 1615, with an introduction by A.L. Rowse, Richmond: the Virginia State Library, 1957, at end of preface, To the Reader.

9. *Narratives of Early Virginia*, p. 11.

10. *Narratives of Early Virginia*, p. 22.

11. Ibid.

12. Edward Maria Wingfield, *A Discourse of Virginia*, edited by Charles Deane, Boston, 1860, available on-line at the website, http://www.virtualjamestown.org/fhaccounts_date.html. See also, Bishop Meade, *Old Churches, Ministers and Families of Virginia*, Vol. 1, Philadephia: J.B. Lippincott Company, 1857, p. 63-64.

13. John Smith, *Advertisements for the Unexperienced Planters of New England, or Anywhere: Or, the Path-Way to Experience to Erect a Plantation*, p. 32. cited in *Pocahontas* by Grace Steel Woodward, University of Oklahoma Press, Norman, 1969, p. 52.

14. Woodward, p. 57. See also Meade, pp. 74-75.

15. Andrews, pp. 77-79. Meade, p. 75, has this prayer and that of end note 14 combined as part of a larger prayer he says was probably prepared by Mr. Crashaw. An expanded version of the prayer in Meade is contained in *For the Colony in Virginea Britannia, Lawes Divine, Morall and Martiall, etc.*, compiled by William Strachey, edited by David H. Flaherty, The University Press of Virginia, Charlottesville, 1969, pp. 93-101. This entire prayer is printed in Appendix 2 of this book.

16. John Smith, *The Generall Historie of Virginia, New-England, and the Summer Isles....*, Book IV, in *Travels and Works of Captain John Smith, Part II*, edited by Edward Arber, Edinburgh: John Grant, 1910, p. 407.

17. See Andrews, pp. 68-71, 77-79.

18. *Memorials of Methodism in Virginia* by W.W.B., 1870, p. 11. Meade, p. 64.

19. John Smith, *Advertisements for the Unexperienced Planters of New England, or Anywhere: Or, the Path-Way to Experience to Erect a Plantation*, cited in *Pocahontas* by Grace Steel Woodward, p. 85.

20. John Smith, *The Generall Historie of Virginia*, edited by Edward Arber, p. 466.

21. John Smith, *A True Relation*, London, 1608, on-line at: http://www.virtualjamestown.org/fhaccounts_date.html

22. See the front of John Smith, *The Generall Historie of Virginia,* edited by Edward Arber, between pages 384 and 385, for a copy of Smith's map of Virginia.

23. John Smith, *A True Relation.* See also Barbour, pp. 165-208. For more references to God, see John Smith, *The Generall Historie of Virginia, New-England, and the Summer Isles....,* Book IV, in *Travels and Works of Captain John Smith, Part II,* edited by Edward Arber, pp. 392, 401, 419, 420, 430.

24. John Smith, *The Generall Historie of Virginia,* edited by Edward Arber, p. 532.

25. Woodward, p. 6.

26. John Smith, *The Generall Historie of Virginia,* edited by Edward Arber, pp. 395-400.

27. Ibid., p. 400.

28. John Smith, *The Generall Historie of Virginia,* edited by Edward Arber, p. 401.

29. Ibid., p. 392.

30. Fiske, p. 111.

31. John Smith, *The Generall Historie of Virginia,* edited by Edward Arber, p. 969.

32. *Nova Britannia*, printed for Samuel Macham, London, 1609, http://www.virtualjamestown.org/fhaccounts_date.html

33. Ibid.

34. John Smith, *The Generall Historie of Virginia,* edited by Edward Arber, p. 497.

35. Ibid., pp. 498-499.

36. Francis B. Simkins, Spotswood H. Jones, and Sidman P. Poole, *Virginia: History, Government, Geography*, Charles Scribners's Sons, New York, 1964, pp. 68-69.

37. Simkins, pp. 69-70; Woodward, p. 125.

38. Woodward, p. 124. Meade, p. 68.

39. Simkins, p. 70.

40. B.F. Morris, *Christian Life and Character of the Civil Institutions of the United States*, p. 93.

41. Meade, p. 76.

42. *A True Discourse of the Present State of Virginia,* p. xi.

43. Meade, p. 73.

44. Ralph Hamor, *A True Discourse of the Present State of Virginia,* Preface to the Reader of the True Discouse.

45. Ibid.

46. Ibid.

47. Ralph Hamor, *A True Discourse of the Present State of Virginia,* pp. 1-2.

48. Ibid., p. 48.

49. Ibid., pp. 48-49.

50. Ibid., p. 50.

51. Woodward, p. 135.

52. *For the Colony in Virginea Britannia, Lawes Divine, Morall and Martiall, etc.,* compiled by William Strachey, edited by David H. Flaherty, The University Press of Virginia, Charlottesville, 1969, pp. ix.

53. Ibid., pp. 10-12.

54. Alexander Whitaker, *Good News from Virginia,* London, 1613, http://www.virtualjamestown.org/fhaccounts_date.html

55. Ibid.

56. Woodward, p. 159.

57. John Rolfe's Letter to Sir Thomas Dale, in *A True Discourse of the Present State of Virginia,* p. 63.

58. Letter from Thomas Dale "to the R. and my most esteemed friend Mr. D.M. at his house at F. Ch. In London," "From Jamestown in Virginia the 18 of June, 1614." in *A True Discourse of the Present State of Virginia,* p. 55-56.

59. Letter from Alex. Whitaker "to my verie deere and loving Cosen M.G. Minister of the B.F. In London," from Virginia, June 18, 1614, in *A True Discourse of the Present State of Virginia,* p. 59-60.

60. Woodward, p. 186.

61. Woodward, p. 191.

62. Simkins, p. 80.

63. *Narratives of Early Virginia,* p. 251.

64. Ibid., p. 260.

65. Ibid., p. 264.

66. http://www.virtualjamestown.org/fhaccounts_date.html

67. Pat Robertson, *America's Dates With Destiny,* Thomas Nelson Publishers, Nashville, 1986, p. 41.

68. John Brinsley, *A Consolation for Our Grammar Schooles,* Scholars' Facsimiles & Reprints, New York, reprinted in 1943 from an original copy in the New York Pubic Library.

69. Simkins, pp. 97-98.

70. *Narratives of Early Virginia,* p. 362, footnote.

71. Simkins, p. 99.

72. John Smith, *The Generall Historie of Virginia, 1624; the Fourth Booke*, in *Narratives of Early Virginia,* p. 22.

Chapter 5

1. See Stephen McDowell, *America, a Christian Nation? Examining the Evidence of the Christian Foundations of America*, Charlottesville: Providence Foundation, 2005.

2. See books published by the Providence Foundation: *America, a Christian Nation; America's Providential History; Building Godly Nations; Defending the Declaration; Contending for the Constitution; America's Providential History, A Documentary Sourcebook; Restoring America's Christian Education;* and other authors such as: David Barton, *Original Intent*, Aledo, Tex.: WallBuilder Press, 2002; Peter Marshall and David Manuel, *The Light and the Glory*, Old Tappan, New Jersey: Fleming H. Revell, 1977; William Federer, *America's God and Country, Encyclopedia of Quotations*, Coppell, Tex.: FAME Publishing, Inc., 1994; various books published by Foundation for American Christian Education, such as *Christian History of the Constitution of the United States, Christian History of the American Revolution.* See also older books, such as: B.F. Morris, *The Christian Life and Character of the Civil Institutions of the United States* (1864), Jesse T. Peck, *The History of the Great Republic, Considered from a Christian Standpoint* (1868), Daniel Dorchester, *Christianity in the United States* (1895).

3. See Donald S. Lutz, "From Covenant to Constitution in American Political Thought," *Publius*, Fall 1980, pp. 101-133.

4. *Colonial Origins of the American Constitution, A Documentary History*, Edited and with an Introductory Essay by Donald S. Lutz, Indianapolis: Liberty Fund, 1998, p. 337.

5. Ibid., p. 32.
6. Ibid., p. 35.
7. Ibid., pp. 36-37.
8. Ibid., pp. 38-39.
9. Ibid., p. 53.
10. Ibid., p. 71.
11. Ibid., pp. 96-97.
12. Ibid., p. 121.
13. Ibid., p. 129.
14. Ibid., p. 163.
15. Ibid., p. 172.
16. Ibid., p. 161.
17. Ibid., p. 189.
18. Ibid., p. 211.
19. Ibid., p. 215.
20. Ibid., pp. 227-228.
21. Ibid., pp. 229-231.
22. Ibid., p. 251.
23. Ibid., pp. 3-4.
24. Ibid., p. 4.
25. Ibid., p. 6-11.
26. *Sources of Our Liberties*, p. 105.
27. *Colonial Origins of the American Constitution, A Documentary History*, pp. 309-313.
28. Ibid., p. 255.
29. Ibid., p. 260.
30. Ibid., p. 263.
31. Ibid., p. 272.
32. Ibid., pp. 272-273.
33. Ibid., p. 281.
34. Ibid., p. 285.
35. Ibid., p. 292.
36. *Significant Documents in United States History*, Vol. 1, 1620-1896, Richard B. Morris, editor, New York: Van Nostrand Reinhold Co., 1969, pp. 39-40.
37. *Colonial Origins of the American Constitution, A Documentary History*, p. 351.

38. Ibid., p. 354.
39. Ibid., p. 361.
40. Ibid., pp. 365-366.

Chapter 6

1. Rev. T. Robert Ingram, *The World Under God's Law*, Houston: St. Thomas Press, 1981, p. 9.

About the Authors

Stephen McDowell, President of the Providence Foundation's Biblical Worldview University, has taught inspiring seminars throughout the United States as well as in Europe, Asia, South America, Australia, and Africa. Since co-founding the Providence Foundation in 1984, he has trained tens of thousands of people from 100 countries, consulted with numerous government officials, assisted in writing political documents and starting political parties, and helped establish classes on godly reformation in numerous churches.

McDowell is the editor of the *Providential Perspective* and has authored and co-authored over a dozen books and videos including *America's Providential History, America a Christian Nation, Building Godly Nations, In God We Trust Tour Guide,* and *Apostle of Liberty: The World-Changing Leadership of George Washington.* His books and writings have been published in 10 different languages. Stephen has appeared on numerous radio and television programs and is a popular speaker at churches, conferences, schools, political groups, and other organizations. Stephen and his wife Beth live in Charlottesville, Virginia, and have four children.

Mark Beliles is President of the International Transformation Network of the Providence Foundation and co-author of many books including *America's Providential History, Liberating the Nations, and Contending for the Constitution.* He has spoken on these topics to millions of people around the world via television and has traveled to consult with leaders in over 20 nations. He has organized several scholarly symposiums, on such topics as Christopher Columbus and "Thomas Jefferson and the Separation of Church and State."

His concern for equipping pastors and Christians to apply Biblical principles to all of life led him to help start the Providence Foundation nearly twenty-five years ago. Mark, who is currently the pastor of Grace Covenant Church in Charlottesville, Virginia, has trained many Christian leaders for the ministry and assisted in establishing churches in America and other nations. Mark and his wife, Nancy, have three children.

The Providence Foundation

The Providence Foundation is a Christian educational organization whose mission is to train and network leaders to transform nations.

The Foundation has been working since its inception in 1983 to fulfill Christ's commission to "make disciples of all nations." According to Bible commentator Matthew Henry, this means to "do your utmost to make the nations Christian nations." Such nations will have transformed people, but also transformed institutions — family, church, education, civil government, business, politics, law, and media.

"Providence" is the preservation, government, guidance, and direction which God exercises over all creation, including the civil affairs of men and women. We disciple nations by teaching all Christ taught. The Scriptures contain a theology of the family, the church, and the state. Principles in God's written Word that relate to civil government, politics, economics, and education are timeless and universally useful for the benefit of any culture on earth today.

The Foundation has focused on principled, Biblical education recognizing such a worldview has historically produced liberty, justice, prosperity, virtue, and knowledge in people and nations.

Through its Biblical Worldview University, the Providence Foundation produces Biblical worldview resources in many languages, offers many types of classes and seminars, trains and certifies instructors to teach others, conducts Christian history tours, and offers speakers for churches, conferences, and seminars. The Foundation's National Transformation Network mentors leaders in education, business, and politics, and encourages others to establish local educational and reformational groups. For more information contact:

Providence Foundation
PO Box 6759
Charlottesville, VA 22906
434-978-4535
Email: info@providencefoundation.com
Website: www.providencefoundation.com

Providence Foundation Resources

Books

America's Providential History (B01) $17.95
How the Lord guided our nation from the very beginning. Proof from history: our nation grew from Christian principles. How to bring them back into the mainstream.

America's Providential History Documentary Sourcebook (B16) $16.95

America's Providential History Teacher's Guide (B17) $16.95

Liberating the Nations (B02) $14.95
God's plan, fundamental principles, essential foundations, and structures necessary to build Christian nations.

Defending the Declaration (B04) $14.95
How the Bible and Christianity influenced the writing of the Declaration.

Watchmen on the Walls (B06) $7.95
The role of pastors in equipping Christians to fulfill their civil duties.

In God We Trust (B03) $14.95
A Christian tour guide for historic sites in Washington D.C., Philadelphia, Jamestown, Williamsburg, Richmond, Mt. Vernon, Charlottesville, and more.

Building Godly Nations (B14) $15.95
The mandate for building Godly nations, lessons from America's Christian history, and how to apply Biblical principles to governing the nations.

Contending for the Constitution (B15) $14.95
Recalling the Christian influence on the writing of the Constitution and the Biblical basis of American law and liberty.

America, a Christian Nation? (B18) $7.95
Examining the evidence of the Christian foundation of America.

In Search of Democracy (B07) $6.95
Foundations, framework, and historical development of biblical government and law.

Independence, Drums of War, vol. 1 (B08) $8.95

Bunker Hill, Drums of War, vol. 2 (B09) $8.95

A Captive in Williamsburg, Drums of War, vol. 3 (B10) $8.95
Drums of War is a series of historical novels for young people designed to teach in an enjoyable way the principles, events, and persons behind America's independence.

The Ten Commandments and Modern Society (B11) $5.95

Restoring America's Christian Education (B12) $5.95

A Guide to American Christian Education (B13) $39.95
Hardback book on the Principle Approach to Education.

The American Dream: Jamestown and the Planting of America (B19) $10.95

Videos/DVD/Game

The Story of America's Liberty (VT01) $19.95
A 60-minute video that looks at the influence of Christianity in the beginning of America, examining principles and providential occurrences.

Dawn's Early Light (VT02) $19.95
A 28-minute version of *The Story of America's Liberty* with up-dated statistics.

The Wall (Video or DVD) (VT03 or DVD01) $15.00
Documentary on the historical roots of "the wall of separation" metaphor.

America: the Game (GM1) $29.95

Audiotape and CD Series

The Christian Roots of America (2 tapes)	(ATS05) (CDS05)	$12.95
Discipling the Nations (4 tapes)	(ATS03) (CDS03)	$24.95
Fundamentals of a Biblical Worldview (8 tapes)	(ATS04) (CDS04)	$49.95
In Search of Democracy (4 tapes)	(ATS02) (CDS02)	$24.95
The Principle Approach to Education for Home or Church Schools (24 tapes)	(ATS01) (CDS01)	$149.95
Liberating the Nations: Developing a Biblical Worldview (7 tapes)	(ATS06) (CDS06)	$44.95

Audiotapes and CDs

America's Freedom: Founded on Faith	(AT15)	(CD15)	$5.95
No Cross, No Crown: Exemplified in the Life of William Penn	(AT1)	(CD1)	$5.95
Reforming the Nations—an Example from the Life of Webster	(AT2)	(CD2)	$5.95
Teaching History from a Providential Perspective	(AT10)	(CD10)	$5.95
The Principle Approach	(AT9)	(CD9)	$5.95
The Principle Approach: Teaching History & Literature	(AT19)	(CD19)	$5.95
God Governs in the Affairs of Men	(AT11)	(CD11)	$5.95
Biblical Economics	(AT7)	(CD7)	$5.95
Honest Money and Banking	(AT8)	(CD8)	$5.95
Biblical Government and Law	(AT5)	(CD5)	$5.95
Forming a Christian Union	(AT6)	(CD6)	$5.95
The Role of Women in History	(AT13)	(CD13)	$5.95
Fundamental Principles of Christian Nations	(AT3)	(CD3)	$5.95
Christ's Teaching on Public Affairs	(AT4)	(CD4)	$5.95
Biblical Principles of Business, Exemplified by McCormick	(AT16)	(CD16)	$5.95
We Hold These Truths—Governmental Principles of Founders	(AT12)	(CD12)	$5.95
American Christian Revolution—Christianity: Fdn. of Liberty	(AT14)	(CD14)	$5.95
Education and the Kingdom of God	(AT17)	(CD17)	$5.95
The Biblical Relationship of Church and State	(AT18)	(CD18)	$5.95
Prophetic Christian Statesmanship	(AT20)	(CD20)	$5.95
The Ten Commandments & Modern Society	(AT21)	(CD21)	$5.95
Why We Celebrate Thanksgiving	(AT27)	(CD27)	$5.95
Qualifications for Godly Officials	(AT26)	(CD26)	$5.95
Thomas Jefferson on "The Foundation of America's Liberty"	(AT28)	(CD28)	$5.95
Jesus: the Focal Point of History	(AT25)	(CD25)	$5.95
Loving God with All Your Mind	(AT24)	(CD24)	$5.95
Fulfilling the Cultural Mandate: How Christians Have Helped Establish God's Kingdom in the Nations	(AT23)	(CD23)	$5.95
Christ the King	(AT22)	(CD22)	$5.95
The Hand of Providence	(AT31)	(CD31)	$5.95
Fast & Thanksgiving Days in Early America	(AT29)	(CD29)	$5.95
Marcus & Narcissa Whitman and the Cultural Mandate	(AT30)	(CD30)	$5.95
Richard Hakluyt & the Providential Colonization of America	(AT31)	(CD31)	$5.95
The Christian Influence in Jamestown and Early Virginia	(AT32)	(CD32)	$5.95

RESPONSE & ORDER FORM

I want to join the Providence Foundation in spreading God's liberty, justice, and prosperity among the nations and restoring to America's homes, churches, and schools the ideas that form the foundation of freedom by becoming a:

☐ **SPECIAL SUPPORTER**: those who contribute any amount toward the ongoing ministry of the Providence Foundation receive the *Providential Perspective* and *Reformation Report*. Enclosed is my gift of:
$ _____

☐ **MEMBER**: those who contribute $100 or more per year receive our newsletters, a 30% discount on all our books, videos, and materials, plus discounts to our Seminars. I will send a regular gift of $_____ per month / quarter / year (circle one). Enclosed is my gift of:
$ _____

I wish to order the following items:

Qty	Title/Product code	Price	Total

	Subtotal
Shipping & Handling:	Member disct. (30%)
* U.S. Mail: $4.00 minimum, 10% if over $35	Sales tax (VA orders add 5%)
* UPS: $5.50 minimum, 12% if over $50.	**Shipping**
(Game orders will be sent UPS)	**TOTAL**
	Contribution
☐ Please send me a Resource Catalog	**GRAND TOTAL**

Method of Payment: ☐ Check/M.O. ☐ VISA ☐ MC ☐ AmEx ☐ Cash

Credit Card No.:_____ Exp. date: _____

Signature:_____

SHIP TO:

Name:_____

Address:_____

City:_____State:____Zip:_____

Phone:(____)_____

Email:_____

Make checks payable to:
Providence Foundation
PO Box 6759
Charlottesville, VA 22906
Phone: 434-978-4535

Also, order by phone or at website
www.providencefoundation.com

How to be a part . . .

I want to be trained and to equip others!

How can the Worldview University serve you?

❐ I would like information on Biblical worldview resources
❐ I am interested in classes via tape, DVD, or online
❐ I want to host a speaker/seminar in my local area
❐ I want certification to be an instructor in my area
❐ I want my church to host university classes
❐ I want to attend a live class in my local area
❐ I want to attend a worldview school in Charlottesville, Virginia
❐ I am interested in serving as an intern in Charlottesville
❐ I would like information on Christian history tours

I want to transform my community!

How can the Transformation Network serve you?

❐ Notify me of upcoming special conferences or events
❐ Enroll me in the online forum/blog with others like me
❐ I want to join the education/media team in my area
❐ I want to join the business/charity team in my area
❐ I want to join the political/legal team in my area
❐ I want certification to be a trainer/mentor in my area
❐ I would like information on investment and giving opportunites toward the work of transformation

If you are a pastor, we believe your role is key in seeing the culture transformed. We especially want to support you in discipling Christians to transform your city. Let us serve you.

❐ I want to financially support the Providence Foundation by becoming
      ❐ Member   ❐ Special supporter
      (Contributors receive our newsletters and other benefits. Please fill out the form on the previous page, or join online: www.providencefoundation.com)

❐ I want to receive your free email communications

Name:_____

Address:_____

City:_____State:_____Zip:_____

Phone:(_____)_____

Email:_____